Bewitched
&
Beguiled

Wolves in Sheep's Clothing

Tracy Hogan

DEDICATION

Father in heaven, I forever bow to You and give thanks for Your eternal love, wisdom, strength, patience and kindness that have enabled me to do that which You ask of me, for I have no natural talents or abilities of my own. King Yeshua, I love Your Authority – I love Your Leadership! I love You forever and always! Forever thank you for the great grace You have given me to complete this book – for apart from You I can do nothing. For being the Author and the Finisher of every page: every word, every revelation, every interpretation, every keystroke, every inspiration, every correction – every re-ordering! For every way You have directed my steps from the beginning to the end, by sending me the Holy Spirit who is the most excellent teacher. For being my strength when I have never been more weak, enabling this work to be complete.

I pray that You Holy Father would be glorified, and that Your Beautiful Son – Yeshua, would be glorified, high and lifted up in these writings as our Savior, Redeemer, Deliverer, Healer, Restorer, Protector, Defender and Provider. That every eternal purpose for why this book has been written, for such a time as this, would be fulfilled and that the Lamb would receive the reward of His suffering in the fullest measure, as He deserves. May the fame of His Great Name, Yeshua, and Your Kingdom increase in each heart that reads these words! AMEN!

ACKNOWLEDGMENTS

With eternal gratitude, I want to thank those who have been a vital part for this book to be written. I could not have done what the Father was asking without each of you.

Chelsea and Christine – my dearest beloved ones, so much that I could say! You are a true joy to labor with in His Vineyards and ones whom this world is truly not worthy of! I always say, He only gives me the best and that could not be a truer statement for both of you! There are no words to adequately thank you for all of your selfless and sacrificial labors of love, prayers and encouragement – always, but especially during this accelerated time of writing. Forever thank you for your always willing hearts, and for all your powerful prayers that gave me the grace to keep moving forward in His plans! I would not have made it without them! Thank you for your faithfulness, focus and commitment to keep the prayer watches going, despite the new levels of 'uncomfortableness' it has brought into your lives. For allowing the Master Potter to mold you and shape you into vessels of His mercy that have been prepared before the foundations of this earth to display His glory. I am in awe of what our Beloved King Yeshua is doing in you and through you, as you keep saying, "Yes" to His ways!

Laura and Caitlyn, forever thank you for all your sacrifices of prayer to hold me up during this season of writing and publishing! This book could not have been written without your powerful prayers and loving sacrifice to do so. Love you dearly!

To my dearly beloved friend Nancy, forever thank you for your love, encouragement and for your eternal friendship. Thank you for your sacrificial labor of love to walk alongside me only encouraging me to go for the 'gold' and for your prayers that I would have the grace to finish well! Your revelatory insights and input have only made these writings much better! This work would not have been complete without you! You are a true friend and a true sister; we have climbed mountains and have walked through the valley of weeping together, pursuing the One we love. Could not imagine traveling this road without you!

And to the one who wished to remain anonymous – forever thank you! Your role was vital and this book would not have been complete without your help! Eternally grateful for your hard labors to make this book better. I love you so!

Mom, forever thank you for your love, encouragement and prayers that pulled me through every time! I could not have written this book without them! You are a true intercessor, who never gives up until and until the breakthrough comes! Eternally thankful the Lord chose you to be my mom – the best mom, a daughter could hope to have! I love you mom! And, to my dearly beloved brothers and family – forever thank you for all your love and prayers! I love you!

Mary, Paschal, Rose, Tony – forever thank you for standing with me. For your hearts of prayer in so many ways, but especially to see this book through to completion. Forever thank you for your kind and loving eternal friendships. You have made my time in Ireland a lot brighter! I am eternally grateful for each of you. You are priceless treasures from heaven – ones who shine brightly in our land that is known as the Emerald Isle.

FOREWORD

It is not often enough that a book like *Bewitched & Beguiled* comes along. While I am sure it is a great read for every follower of Christ, but if one is comfortable with one's "Evangelical walk with God," this may not be the read for you. Why? It will open one's eyes to the reality that the spirit world is more real that the physical realm. The awareness that we do not wrestle with flesh and blood will pierce through and challenge one's religious slumber.

If you are comfortable with your faith being an ancillary component to a cultural lifestyle that is focused on "self-betterment," again, this may not be the book for you. Reason? As this is read, you will quickly understand God's intended purpose for you personally, and His call to His Bride (The Church) to be ready for the Bridegroom (Jesus).

This book will not be for the faint of heart due to the depth of content and biblical support, so time must be spent to prayerfully process, and absorb this spiritual information. While some of the concepts may initially challenge your thinking, it will expand your understanding of how the enemy works to trip up the believer and even thwart God's desire for us to live in the secret places of intimacy with the Father. The examples of different ministries, observations, and critiques are done with humility and grace.

The content in this read was far beyond informational, by being rich with practical steps to walk a life of humility and a life of being set apart for His service. There is hope in these pages that confirms that even though there are attempts by the adversary to destroy the believer, you and I are to be more than conquerors through Christ.

Over the last 10 years I have had the honor and privilege to observe Tracy Hogan's life as she has passionately pursued her calling. Her commitment to prayer, worship, and the deep study of God's word has produced a sweet incense to the Master as she bends low in humility. It is with confidence that I know the inward work of God's Holy Spirit in Tracy's life has produced this truly anointed work that will be a great teaching tool for personal growth, Christian education in the local church, and in academia.

REV. PAUL D.M JOHNSON D. MIN.
The Gathering Place Church
Phoenix, Arizona, USA

In an era of dark in Ireland in 433 AD, it is spoken Saint Patrick burned a light testifying to the Resurrection of Christ under penalty of death; over 100 plus years later the song "Be Thou My Vision" was written to honor his testimony to shine for the Lord Jesus Christ against a king's decree exalting false deities. In St. Patrick's journals, his own words reveal his love and perseverance for Jesus Christ who had called him forth in love. Not only in Ireland now but on the earth, Tracy is a life and light set apart. Literally a moment before Tracy reached out to me to ask if I would write an endorsement, I had just thought of her and said, *"She is one of whom the world is not worthy."* Then when I saw the title of this book, I knew how intense and important this assignment is in this hour on earth: to address the Church called to be holy out of all darkness within her – specifically now the crafted darkness to destroy faith, the infrastructure of the soul, and the very creation destined for glory, from within. Tracy exhorts the Body of Christ in the same call as Jude the apostle, *"Mercy, peace, and love be multiplied to you. Beloved, although I was very eager to write to you about our common salvation, I found it necessary to write appealing to you to contend for the faith that was once for all delivered to the saints"* [Jude 1:2-3].

One could only write a book like this at the request of the Lord, as one who has lived through these trenches of wickedness, and as one who has humbly, valiantly wept, suffered, and submitted to the Lord of Glory and the Lamb Who is Majestic in Holiness. She weeps, suffers, and submits still. As one who seeks Him as her vision, Tracy here exposes the predatory and stealth nature of witchcraft advancing within the Church on earth to destroy. Our Lord does warn us that at the end of the age it is so – deception blinding so many. At the call of the Good Shepherd, she too shepherds and calls out, *"Behold, the Bridegroom comes."*

There are some whom the Lord chooses to walk through certain aspects of dark realms with Him, and these must hold Him ever nearest and dearest to them for very life as they follow Him through this terrain. He leads them through these particular valleys of the shadow of death because He has assignments to destroy demonic fortress strongholds which bring harm of rebellion. Tracy has written so transparently in the active voice and context of her own love story to further draw the beloved into the great love story of God in Christ. It is in this place He has asked her to pen these words and stand against this evil in our midst and any to which a soul has ascribed, knowingly or unknowingly. A fragrance fills the air when Tracy lifts her voice in prayer, and she walks in this Love that has His immortal rod of light in her: Christ the Radiance of the Father, Christ Who alone shatters the enchanted mysteries and power of darkness, Jesus Christ The Son Who loves us and washes us from our sin – our darkness for which we repent – by His Blood, Christ our Joy and First Love, Jesus Christ Who is the Resurrection and the Life. Our God is light: in Him is no darkness at all, nor shadow of turning, and never shall dark remain before the Lord of Glory.

Love never fails; these three abide forever faith, hope, and love, and the greatest of these is love [1 Corinthians 13:8a,13].

NANCY C. DEWIND
Your sister in Christ

Our dear Sister has written a wonderful book on a very needful subject. This is a serious problem inside the Church which most if not all Christians and leaders are either ignorant or in denial or are inadvertently influenced to act likewise. This book will help to educate the Church and help it to be pure and spotless.

SADHU SUNDAR SELVARAJ
Jesus Ministries

I am happy to recommend Tracy's latest book *Bewitched and Beguiled*. It is an urgent wake-up call to a slumbering Church and I include myself in that category. I am reminded of Paul's final words to the Ephesians in Acts 20:28-30 about savage wolves coming in among the flock after his departure. She does not suggest we become over judgmental or critical, but to earnestly seek the discernment of the Spirit, and be guided by the Word at all times. Pray for discernment as you read this book.

We need to realise that we are in a spiritual battle once we accept Jesus as our Savior and Lord. Justification is instant, but if we really desire to become the Bride of Christ we must press on, and yield to the sanctifying and transforming work of the Holy Spirit, and persevere to the end. This is not a journey for the lukewarm or halfhearted. Jesus has given His all for us, and if we really appreciated how much He has done for us, we would give our all for Him, no matter how painful or costly.

Tracy shares her own struggles and battles with a humility and honesty that is both admirable, inspirational and very instructive. We need to recognise how the enemy seeks to steal, kill and destroy by sowing division in so many diverse and unexpected ways. Read it prayerfully and be wonderfully blessed!

PASCHAL COFFEY
Cork, Ireland

As I read Tracy's book, *Bewitched and Beguiled*, the United States is presently being inundated by a movement that appears to be innocent in nature. But behind it are people who openly worship Satan and stand for the dismantling of the family. With their own words they openly call for the spirits of their ancestors – those who have died, to help them in their cause. They declare with their words that the phrase 'Black Lives Matter' is a movement powered by ancestral spirits, where they call upon the name of those who have been killed, and other names – the names of demon gods.

Many in our society today are merely pawns that are being fueled by ignorance from our past and lies concerning our future.

Unfortunately, the worship of Baal and Balak have entered our churches because the watchers are not watching and the intercessors are not praying, and because these powers of darkness are being fueled by the blood of aborted babies.

My dearest brothers and sisters what you are our seeing in our nation and churches is not just the deeds of humans. It is the influence of powerful spirits using the flesh of men through what the scriptures call witchcraft. It is unfolding into several perfect storms: political, financial, social and mental. As you read our dear Sister's book exposing Satan's ways through witchcraft in the Church, I pray that our Father in heaven will give you insight not only to know that you are called and expected to engage in this spiritual battle, but how to fight against this evil that wants to destroy our faith and God's plans for us.

DR. EUGENE UNDERWOOD
Spirit Life Ministries,
Special Forces School of Ministries
Anchorage, Alaska, USA

Contents

WOLVES IN SHEEP'S CLOTHING

Have you at times felt paralysed, suffocated, strangulated and immobilised in doing the will of God in your life? Particularly, when pressing in during your times of prayer? Or, perhaps, have you experienced a great battle to even get to that place of prayer? Have you had relationships in your personal life, in your church or ministry seem like overnight they have fallen apart with no hope of restoration in sight?

This book is written to and for the Body of Christ to look at a topic that most in the Church fear to talk about for many reasons. One being many believe that as a new creation in Christ we cannot be influenced, manipulated and controlled by the dark and wicked, occultic powers known as witchcraft. It is written to help shed light on a topic that is rarely discussed from behind the pulpit, in our ministry meetings, or during the different Christian conferences that we attend, wanting to gain spiritual growth and healing.

It is a subject matter that as a believer in Christ, we need not fear. Instead, we must educate ourselves on the reality of theses powers of darkness that rage constantly trying to stop us from fulfilling the call that is on our lives. For ultimately, they want to stop us from fulfilling the high and lofty destiny that the Lord Jesus Christ has for us – to be the Bride of Christ. A Bride who will be found without spot or wrinkle. One who will be equally yoked to the Bridegroom King in word, thought and deed, and one who will rule and reign with Him over all of creation through the Millennium Reign, into the Eternal Kingdom Age for all of eternity [Ephesians 5:27, 1 John 2:6, Revelation 20:6, 22:5].

This is not another book on spiritual warfare. Although, in some ways it could be portrayed that way. For whenever Light exposes darkness it must flee; that in itself is a form of spiritual warfare. This book's sole purpose is to help equip the true Church – the Bride of Christ for the dark days that are only getting darker. It is written on the foundation of the Holy Scriptures and by sharing my personal experiences, as well as others, that are taking place in the Body of Christ today.

The writings in this book are not to glorify Satan and his very real seat of dark powers, but to unseat them, so that we may be as wise as serpents and as harmless as doves. That we may put on the full armor of God that we may stand against the evil that wants to destroy the works our Father has sent us to this earth to complete. This evil tries to destroy our minds, our wills, our emotions, our physical bodies, our families, our marriages and the God ordained eternal relationships that were formed in our lives for the advancement of His Kingdom. These dark powers operate to destroy cities, communities and nations, trying to stop destinies from being fulfilled individually, and as nations.

We are all called to resist the devil that he may flee [James 4:7]. I ask the question: how many in the Church today even believe that there is a devil? I have heard some truly astounding words spoken over the years from professed believers in Christ who do not believe Satan, or his dark powers against us, are real.

Or, if we do believe these dark powers exist, then let me ask how many Christians believe that the Lord Jesus requires and expects us to resist Satan's tactics, so that he will flee from our lives and the sphere of influences we have each been given to advance His Kingdom?

If we do believe this is what the Lord requires from us, I then ask: how many in the Church today are putting on the whole armor of God that we would stand against the wiles of the devil that we may stand in the evil day [Ephesians 6:11, 13]? How many are staying alert, sober minded and watching for when the enemy comes roaring like a lion to devour God's plans in our lives, by trying to steal, kill and destroy those plans any way he can [1 Peter 5:8, John 10:10]?

The truth of the matter is that most are not. Most Christians believe we do not have to engage in fighting the good fight of faith in this arena. If that were true though, why would Paul exhort us to fight the good fight of faith? Why would he warn and exhort us if there was not a real battle raging against us, trying to stop faith from working its end result in our lives, the salvation of our souls [1 Timothy 6:12, 1 Peter 1:9]?

Faith without works is dead works. As a new creation in Christ, we have very real Kingdom assignments. We are to complete the works that our Father in heaven has sent us to this earth to complete for the advancement of His Kingdom, on earth as it exists in heaven. The number one work that we have all been assigned to complete is to be transformed into the image and likeness of the Lord Jesus, until Christ has been completely conformed within us – until the full stature of Christ is within our soul [Galatians 4:19, Ephesians 4:13]. To the degree that we are being transformed into His likeness, meaning becoming like His character in our words, thoughts and deeds, will determine how well we complete our other Kingdom assignments. Meaning, are we doing them His way or our way? Is it my will or His will?

Equally, to the degree that we are willing to crucify our flesh, by living a holy, pure and consecrated life unto the Lord, will determine to what degree we will or will not be deceived. The more we are being conformed into His character, by going through the trials and afflictions that come into our lives His way – by denying ourselves, taking up our cross and following the Lamb wherever He may lead, the less likely we will be deceived. If we are not willing to die – crucify our flesh – to our pride, ambition, jealousy, gossip, unforgiveness, rejection, our reputation as some examples, then our flesh and our unsaved soul will lead us astray every time. We will be vessels ripe for deception that will cloud our vision and dull our hearing.

The end result of our faith was always meant to bring us into the fullness of our salvation, where our souls are completely saved – purified 100% with His Refiner's fire, that we may become the Bride of Christ [1 Peter 1:9, Isaiah 48:10, James 1:21, Revelation 3:16-18, 19:7-8]. Getting saved was just the beginning of our transformation – not the end result.

Satan not only fears a praying remnant, but greatly fears the Bride of Christ maturing and coming into the fullness of her rightful inheritance and identity that can only be found in Christ. It is He, Who, by the indwelling of the Holy Spirit, will equip her with everything she needs – overflowing with the Seven Spirits of the Lord, to be used mightily in these last days, and to bring in the final great harvest [Isaiah 11:2].

The enemy knows that once the Bride of Christ has made herself ready, it will be his dismissal once and for all – hallelujah [Revelation 19:7, 20:10]! So, he comes to steal, kill and destroy any way he can those works in our lives that are meant to transform us, by one degree of glory to the next, to be like the Lord Jesus. Satan ruthlessly preys on our weaknesses, wounds and the sin in our lives to use them against us. His goal is to stop us from obtaining the end result of our faith.

One main way that Satan accomplishes this is through the powers of witchcraft that are operating in the Church today. This is not a new tactic, but one that has existed since the fall of man. Some displays of witchcraft in the Church today are easier to identify – Harry Potter, Destiny Card readings, Halloween parties under the guise of a 'harvest party.' Most crafting's though, are not so obvious and are done in secret, and these practitioners come into our churches, ministries and meetings as wolves disguised in sheep's clothing.

My prayer is this book will reveal, uncover and unmask some of the many masks that these workers of darkness hide behind, while at the same time empower believers in Christ to contend for their faith like their lives depend upon it because they do! This is not an exhaustive revealing on this subject matter, only what the Lord Jesus has allowed me to experience over the years, now wanting me to share with His beloved ones to help us not to be bewitched and beguiled anymore.

The Lord wants none of us to be deceived. In this late hour we are seeing an increase of witches and warlocks in our church services, ministries and prayer meetings. We are seeing the false prophets, false teachers and false anointings on the rise – all coming as wolves dressed in sheep's clothing.

I pray this book will bless you, strengthen you, encourage you and build you up in every way the enemy has tried to destroy and tear you down. May His Light expose the darkness that wants to destroy you, causing it to flee! May His Light bring redemption and restoration in the areas of your life that have been polluted, defiled, affected and infected by these workers of darkness. That which Satan meant for evil, may the Lord Jesus turn and work it for your good – all to the Lamb's glory! AMEN!

____

CHAPTER 1

____

A BATTLE OF GOOD AGAINST EVIL

____

The devil, who deceived them, was cast into the lake of fire and brimstone where the beast and the false prophet are. And they will be tormented day and night forever and ever. But the cowardly, unbelieving, abominable, murderers, sexually immoral, sorcerers, idolaters, and all liars shall have their part in the lake which burns with fire and brimstone, which is the second death [Revelation 20:6, 21:8].

Just as the Lord Jesus Christ is the same yesterday, today and forever, Satan's power is real and he comes to kill, steal and destroy. But one day soon, he will be forever bound up in hell no longer able to inflict his horrific evils upon mankind, and all of His creation any more.

Until then, as believers in the Lord Jesus, we are in a real battle – a battle of good against evil. Light against darkness. Truth against lies and deception. A battle not against flesh and blood, but a battle against principalities, powers, rulers of the darkness and spiritual hosts of wickedness in the heavenly places [Ephesians 6:12].

Since the fall of man, Satan has been able to deceive mankind. He often does this by finding a human vessel to partner with him to promote his evil agenda that rages against the Kingdom of God. There are multiple ways the enemy comes to steal, kill and destroy in our lives, but I am focusing primarily in this book on those that are known as workers of darkness – witches, wizards, warlocks, Satanists – children of the devil, that have infiltrated the Church as wolves in sheep's clothing.

They come to practice their witchcraft – their magic, their spells, curses, hexes, vexes, jinxes, mantras, lotions, potions, charms, oils, fetishes, feathers, unholy candle lightings, satanic rituals, blood sacrifices, E.S.P., astral projection and many other occultic powers and practices on the vulnerable, and often unaware believer.

Why do they do this? I cannot answer that fully. But one thing is certain, in their current unsaved state, they hate God and everything He stands for – so they come with one purpose: to destroy. They allow their bodies, which are created in God's image – meant to be pure and holy, to be used as the ultimate insult to the Creator. By becoming a channel of the most profane kind, they enable Satan to display his hate and outright rebellion towards the Most High through them.

They come to destroy our faith, faithfulness and obedience to the Word of God. To destroy our relationship with the Lord, if possible. Our obedience was always meant to restore us back to an intimate love relationship with the Lord Jesus, and our Father in heaven. Our obedience is vital if we are to reach the end result of our faith – to be conformed into His likeness. Our obedience will lead us into seasons or situations that make our flesh uncomfortable.

But the Lover of our soul cares more that we learn to become 'comfortable' with being 'uncomfortable' in what He asks of us. Why? Because He is after the transformation of our soul, that will restore us back to an intimate relationship with Him. Being comfortable in our flesh – our ways of doing things, will bring us to a place of stagnation in our walk. That is unsatisfying to Him and to us. He desires more than we do, that we grow and mature in His ways.

So, these workers of darkness come to destroy God's redemptive plan for mankind to be restored back to an intimate relationship with the Lord. A relationship whose foundation is built on truth, purity, holiness and the fear of the Lord. They come to destroy the Seed that has been placed within our spiritual womb – wanting to cause one spiritual miscarriage after another. They try to stop the fruit that is to come forth from His Seed – a Bride who will be fully matured. One who has been conformed into the very character of Christ – a Bride who has made herself ready for the Wedding Supper of the Lamb [Revelation 12:5, 19:7-9].

Some of these workers of darkness have been born into the 'craft' from one generation to the next. It is all that they know. Most, though, have chosen this path of evil for whatever reasons in their lives. May God have mercy on their souls and may they be saved, we pray! So, we do not hate the people. But we do hate the darkness and destruction that their evil works represent, while remembering that we do not wrestle against flesh and blood.

At the same time, as believers in Christ we must stand against this evil. We need to know this evil is not going to flee without us enforcing the victory of the Cross. We enforce that victory by loving and pursing truth more than we love our own lives. By coming out of all compromise. By learning to walk low before God and before man. By living a consecrated life of purity and holiness. By living a lifestyle of intercessory prayer where we know how to effectively wield the sword of the Spirit, every day! We would do well to remember what Jude said:

> **JUDE 1:18-19, 23 AMP.**
> *That in these last days there will be scoffers who seek to gratify their own unholy desires, following after their own ungodly passions. It is these who are agitators, setting up distinctions and causing divisions – merely sensual, devoid of the Holy Spirit and destitute of any higher spiritual life – strive to save others, snatching them out of the fire, on others take pity but with fear, loathing even the garment spotted by the flesh and polluted by their sensuality.*

Spirit of Complacency

In the summer of 2016, while preparing to do our first ministry meeting in Ireland, the word of the Lord came to me one morning while in prayer. The Lord exhorted me, *"Pray against a spirit of complacency that has dulled the spirit of His people."* At the time, I thought I understood what complacency meant, but because this became a direct prayer strategy from the Lord, I wanted to look further into its meaning, so that we could pray effectively.

Complacency can be defined as: a feeling of self-satisfaction, being unaware of the dangers and deficiencies within a person and all around them – having a feeling of false security.[1]

When Paul was speaking to the Galatians, he was not speaking to unsaved people. He was speaking to believers, when he asked who has bewitched or cast a spell over you.

> **GALATIANS 3:1 AMP.**
> *O you poor and silly and thoughtless and unreflecting and senseless Galatians!* **Who has fascinated or bewitched or cast a spell over you,** *unto whom — right before your very eyes — Jesus Christ was openly and graphically set forth and portrayed as crucified?*

Now, let us look at the definition of bewitched and beguiled to help better understand how a person might become unaware of the dangers and deficiencies regarding witchcraft, not only within our own lives, but within the Body of Christ – in our homes, churches and meetings.

Definition of Bewitched

Bewitched can be defined as: controlled or affected by or as if by a magic spell to influence, attract, charm, entice, lure, seduce or tempt.[2]

Other words related to bewitched: spellbound, entranced, enchanted, cursed, jinxed, hexed, possessed, mesmerized, bedazzled and captivated.

The opposite of bewitched is: blessed, favored, restored and free.

Definition of Beguiled

Beguiled can be defined as: to attract or delight as if by magic to cause someone to believe what is untrue.[3]

Other words related to beguiled: baited, allured, betrayed, conned, deceived, deluded, duped, entrapped, ensnared, trapped, hoodwinked, misguided, misled, snookered, strung along, tricked, cheated, defrauded, fleeced and swindled.

The opposite of beguiled is: exposed, revealed, uncloaked, uncovered, unmasked and unveiled.

How Do We Define Witchcraft?

How do we define witchcraft? In its simplest form it is someone forcing their will upon another. This can be done with the black and white magic that is practiced by these workers of darkness, and their different crafts as mentioned earlier. For example: a witch can create a love potion that would cause a man to desire another woman, causing him to divorce his wife and marry another. Many divorces in the Church are a direct result of witchcraft. That may be hard for some to hear, but it is a sad reality.

I know of a couple who were strong Christians for over 30+ years when their lives were devastated by witchcraft. The husband's job required that he travel a few months during the year and his wife was not always able to join him. There was a woman who worked for his company, who often placed her hand on his shoulder, against his wishes. At one point, this woman took his hairbrush out of his hotel room. It was nothing that he or his wife could ever prove, but they were aware that this woman's motive towards them was not good, but to harm them.

They had discerned that the powers operating from this woman were witchcraft, and she was using the hair from his hairbrush to put spells and curses on him. Her goal was to destroy his anointing, by trying to entrap him in sexual sin. But neither of them had that understanding at the time, only that her intentions were to do them harm.

If you doubt such things are possible, remember Samson and Delilah. Delilah may not have been a witch, but the secret to Samson's anointing and great strength to be a mighty man of war for the Lord was in his hair. He was a Nazarite who was dedicated to God from the womb. One of the Nazarite's vows is that they do not cut their hair.

Samson was seduced by Delilah. She was assigned to betray him to his enemies, the Philistines, who feared him and wanted to destroy him. With her beguiling speech to seduce and deceive Samson, Delilah learns the secret of his strength: if his head was ever shaved, he would become as weak as any man. Delilah entraps him and shaves his head. So after a few fleeting moments of sexual lust, Samson lost the anointing that was on his life – the Lord departed. He never recovered it; instead, he became blind and imprisoned [Judges 16].

Isn't that just what sin does? It separates us from God, causing us to become blind and imprisoned to it. Often, though, there are real powers of darkness causing this to happen.

So, back to this couple. Soon their marriage began having more problems than normal. Both were being affected by these powers of darkness, causing pride, anger, bitterness and unforgiveness to drive them further apart. The husband eventually committed adultery, and soon afterwards divorced his wife, later telling people that God told him to do so!

Clearly, he had been bewitched and beguiled, becoming blinded to the Word of God. God would not tell someone to do something He hates [Malachi 2:16]. Even though the wife did not want a divorce, he was not willing to reconcile, nor hear any counsel to that effect. He was listening to a false voice that became his reality. But at that point, after the sexual sin had been committed, it had become impossible to reason with him and that witch had succeeded in her mission. She had preyed on this man's weakness, who had a previous history of sexual sin that had not been fully healed and set free from. It is why she was able to hex and bait him into sexual sin with the goal to destroy the call on his life. To this day this man has not walked in the anointing that he once had. That is the goal of these workers of darkness – to stop the plans of God from being fulfilled in our lives.

Witchcraft Prayers

Another way witchcraft can affect our lives, is when Christians, who are not involved in the occult, but pray what I call 'witchcraft prayers.' This is when a believer prays against another person's will. For example: someone they know may be called by God to move to another city. They do not want this to happen for whatever reasons – they may miss the person greatly, or they do not believe the person heard from God correctly.

Therefore, they pray for this move to not happen – for obstacles to come that would prevent it from happening. They are not a worker of darkness, and they are not intentionally trying to be evil, but all the same, our words have power to create. Our words either bring life or death [Proverbs 18:21]. Satan cannot create anything. He can only re-create from that which has already been created. So he can get a hold of these prayers and cause havoc in a believer's life.

PROVERBS 18:21 AMP.
Death and life are in the power of the tongue, and they who indulge in it shall eat the fruit of it [for death or life].

So, in this situation, when a Christian prays for that move to not happen, those words become accessible to the enemy, where he can now create from what has been spoken. He will use those prayers against the believer who is to move, by bringing situations into their life, trying to stop the move from taking place. Trying to cause them to be out of the will of God. It is why they are called 'witchcraft prayers.' Because they are prayers against another person's will. God will never go against our will, and why it is so important that we do not pray against another person's will, even though our heart is not trying to hurt them.

Biblical Origins of Witchcraft

In Genesis 9-11, we see the first instances of slavery, anti-Semitism and witchcraft with Nimrod and the Tower of Babel.

> ### GENESIS 10:10 AMP.
> *He was a mighty hunter before the Lord; therefore it is said, like Nimrod a mighty hunter before the Lord. The beginning of his kingdom was Babel, Erech, Accad, and Calneb, in the land of Shinar [in Babylonia].*

In Hebrew, the name Nimrod means 'we will revolt.' Furthermore, the phrase "A mighty hunter before the Lord," actually reads in Hebrew, "He was a mighty hunter in defiance of the Lord – hunting the souls of men."[4]

Nimrod was the founder of Babylon, and he warred against Shem. Shem, Ham and Japheth were the sons of Noah. It was through Shem's lineage that the Seed of Christ, our Lord Jesus was birthed. Nimrod was also the grandson of Ham. Ham is the root of the Hebrew word *'Hamas,'* which means 'violence.' It is where the terrorist group Hamas get their name from.

So, because Ham did not honor his father Noah when he saw his nakedness, a curse came upon Canaan his son, who was Nimrod's uncle. Can we start to see the family dynamics? How a 'family rivalry' of great evil began long ago with Nimrod warring against his own blood relations and the plans God had for them, birthing the origins of anti-Semitism.

It is of interest to note the two different lineages or 'seeds' that are birthed with Shem and Ham. We see one of Christ [Noah, Shem, Abraham], and the other of anti-Christ [Ham, Cush, Nimrod]. Scripture is not exactly clear, but seems to indicate that the 'seed' of the anti-Christ has its origins from the lineage of Ham.

Nimrod would have practiced the worship of the Canaanites, known as Sun worship. Their worship was wicked, and rooted in sensuality and temple prostitution. The Chaldeans built altars to the fertility gods of Baal and Ashtoreth, where their priests offered homosexual acts – spilling their seed in the temple as an offering, along with human sacrifices to those gods. It was deeply steeped in witchcraft, sorcery, divination, soothsaying and fortune telling. It angered the Lord greatly.

JEREMIAH 19:4-5
Because they have forsaken Me and made this an alien place, because they have burned incense in it to other gods whom neither they, their fathers, nor the kings of Judah have known, and have filled this place with the blood of the innocents (they have also built the high places of Baal, to burn their sons with fire for burnt offerings to Baal, which I did not command or speak, nor did it come into My mind).

We see that Nimrod builds the Tower of Babel to directly oppose God. Its construction was the beginning of his kingdom in the land of Shinar. The laborers would have been a part of Nimrod's kingdom, and they would not have any other choice but to build it. Therefore, this is where slavery gets its origins, as it was forced labor. At that time, the whole earth was of one language and Nimrod wanted to rule over it by building a city and a tower that reaches to the heavens, wanting to make a name for himself [Genesis 11:1-4].

So, how would Nimrod do this and succeed? We see the answer in Genesis 11:4.

GENESIS 11:4
And they said, "Come, let us build ourselves a city, and **a tower whose top is in the heavens**; *let us make a name for ourselves, lest we be scattered abroad over the face of the whole earth."*

By building the Tower of Babel, Nimrod was able to create an open portal that reached the heavens, giving the hordes of demons and fallen angels who dwell in the second heavens – Satan's realm of authority, free access to defile the earth and destroy God's plans for mankind. We see the scriptural foundation for an open portal in the heavens, in the dream Jacob had while fleeing from Esau's presence.

GENESIS 28:12

"Then he dreamed, and behold a ladder was set up on the earth, and its top reached to heaven; and there the angels of God were ascending and descending on it."

We see an open heavens, where angels ascend and descend. This is a biblical and earthly reality that God uses to advance His plans on earth. Open portals are gateways into the eternal realm, and as a believer in the Lord Jesus, we are seated with Him in heavenly places. Therefore, we have access to these heavenly portals, for one of their purpose is to help us fulfill our destinies [Ephesians 2:6].

GENESIS 28:16-17

When Jacob awoke from his sleep and said, "Surely the Lord is in this place, and I did not know it." And he was afraid and said, "How awesome is this place! This is none other than the house of God, and this is the gate of heaven!"

Equally, though, Satan has open portals that provide access to his realm of authority, which is in the second heavens. These portals enable him to unleash his demons, fallen angels, principalities, powers, rulers of the darkness and spiritual wickedness in heavenly places to work his evil on this earth, and in our lives.

The Tower of Babel was one of these open portals. Satan cannot create anything new, but he can re-create from that which exists. Nimrod used this spiritual reality and principle for evil, to rebel against God, by accessing the fallen angels and demons to influence the inhabitants on the earth into his way of thinking, wanting to rule the world.

It is why the judgment of God came upon it – it was so wicked and corrupt! The Lord confused their language and scattered them from that place upon the earth, so they could not unite and destroy His eternal plans for mankind. Therefore, we see one of the earliest displays of witchcraft taking place in the land of Shinar, also known as Babel or Babylon.

Seducing Spirits and Fallen Angels

Today, Jezebel with the spirit of Babylon and the spirit of harlotry, have rampantly infiltrated the Church with seducing demons and fallen angels, causing the masses to follow after doctrines of demons. They are trying to take over by creating a new set of rules, or standards for Christians to follow. What we are seeing is nothing less than apostasy.

At large, the Church is full of compromise, mixture and temple prostitution. We have lost the fear of the Lord and what it means to be holy as He is holy. We see many flocking to churches and ministries that are merchandising the gifts and anointing, with their lying signs and wonders, or to those who promote a false grace with unbalanced prosperity teachings, that are void of the forewarnings of the judgment of God and our need to repent of our sin. We see the LGBTQ+ agenda demanding that it have equal rights, with more gay pastors in the pulpit than ever before.

We love the people, but we hate the sin that destroys our relationship with the Lord, His ways for us and His Sanctuary. The wages of sin are death – it does not matter what sin it is. If we do not repent and turn away from it, meaning leave it behind, and be cleansed with the blood of the Lamb, we will reap an eternal consequence of death. That is not the Lord Jesus' desire or will for anyone. He is longsuffering towards our sin nature, that none should perish, that we would instead all repent and receive eternal life [Romans 6:23, 2 Peter 3:9].

EPHESIANS 2:1-2
And you He made alive, who were dead in trespasses and sins, in which you once walked according to the course of this world, according to the prince of the power of the air, the spirit who now works in the sons of disobedience.

What most do not realise is that our sin nature is being influenced by Satan's realm of authority with his demons and fallen angels, which are coming into our homes, work places, churches and ministry meetings. Satan sends them to prey on our weaknesses and wounds, enabling them to delude and blind us to our sin, if he can. If we have unconfessed sin in our lives – bitterness, jealousy, greed, Satan has legal right to harass us this way. Or, if we have wounds that have not been healed, we will end up listening to another voice, that is not the Good Shepherd's voice. Examples: the voice of rejection, self-pity, shame, fear, to name just a few.

About two years ago, the Lord allowed me to have a dream that depicts this very real scenario. I had been praying for the Lord to confirm if I was to write this book on witchcraft. He had given me a very vivid and clear dream a few weeks prior, where it would have been hard to misinterpret. But not feeling at all qualified to write on this topic, knowing there are many more qualified with greater experience, I was asking Him to confirm that I understood His plan correctly.

Dream: Meeting with Witchcraft

In the dream, I was with my ministry partner and we were on our way to attend a ministry meeting. It was night time and in a location that was not known to me. When we arrived, a woman came to meet us in the reception area. She had something really odd in her hand and was putting it around my ministry partner's neck. It was invasive and overwhelming, and my ministry partner pulled away immediately.

The woman stopped for a few moments, stood in front of her, and then started to do it again. But before she could, I took my right arm and hand and standing to the side of her, I slugged her really hard in the middle of her stomach with something that I was holding in my hand. It was not clear what was in my hand. It was not a hard object, but soft. But the blow to her was really hard. In the natural it would not make sense.

This blow took this woman by surprise and knocked any notion out of her to do that again to my ministry partner. She walked away, heading into the meeting room. I turned to my ministry partner saying, *"I am not so sure I should have done that."* She replied, *"Oh no, that was a really anointed hit!"* It was known that this woman was not happy with me, and at her first opportunity would retaliate against me. It was also known that she was somehow connected to and responsible for facilitating the meeting, and that she knew the man who was speaking very well.

On our way to go in, I sensed that it was not good for me to go into the meeting. The door was open, and I could see there were a few people in the room talking. I could see the man who was doing the meeting near the front talking to a small group of people.

There was some activity taking place in the room, and it caused me to want to stay. Then things changed. It was now looking like no one else was going to stay. I had discerned it was not good for me to be in this meeting with this man, for he wanted to do me harm.

My ministry partner and I quickly left. When we were just about out the door, two things happened at the same time. First, the meeting was no longer empty but full of people, and it was known that this group of people were involved in compromise, mixture, various sins, and were at different levels in their walk and maturity. This was known to me because they had large white placards in front of their stomachs that revealed what they were involved in. It was a title, written in black on each of their placards. One had compromise written on their placard, another had pride, someone else jealousy, another liar, gossip, bitterness, division, rejection, self-pity. On and on. They were unaware that their sin, or wounds, were hanging on their sleeves, so to speak, for all to see. They were all happy and chatting with one another in their deceived state.

The second thing that took place, simultaneously, as we entered into the reception area from the meeting room, was that out of nowhere, about seven or eight bigger than life, horrific demons manifested right before our eyes. They were about twelve feet tall. They had the bodies of humans but their faces were animal like – yet wicked and contorted, some like masks. Some had horns. They were heading into the meeting that was now taking place. I could see them, but those in the meeting room were blinded to them. They were blinded to how the enemy was using their sin or wounds and influencing them to follow a false voice – the man who was doing the meeting. These demons, or fallen angels were sent to influence the Christians in that meeting, with the purpose to stop them from fulfilling their destiny, by using their various sins or wounds, which were written on their placards.

As we walked by these horrible creatures, and quickly left the building, I said to my ministry partner, as if what we had just seen was 'normal' and said matter of fact, *"That's from witchcraft and we need to get used to it, because that is what we are going to be contending with in these days."* Once outside the building, I see a beloved sister from another ministry that I respect very much. She is talking with a man and she is not very happy. She looks at me and says, *"That what just happened was from witchcraft."* End of dream.

Interpretation of Dream

There is a lot of interpretation to this dream. What I want to mainly highlight is that the man doing the meeting represents a false prophet or teacher operating under a false anointing. The woman who met us, and was connected with this false teacher who was responsible for organising the meeting, represents Jezebel. It is why she went for my ministry partner's neck. She was trying to silence her voice. She went for the one who she thought was weaker and more vulnerable to destroy. By going after my ministry partner, she was also attempting to destroy the ministry. By trying to destroy those who are called to be a part of this work. For the ministry represents the true prophetic voice, and Jezebel comes to destroy and silence that voice, and anyone associated with it.

I believe that what was in my hand, was the 'sword of the spirit' – the Word of God. This is why it was such an anointed, direct hit – a death blow, so to speak, that exposed this woman's counsel. Why it is vital to be grounded in the Word of God, for it will not only protect us in these last days from the false prophets, teachers and anointings – but will expose their evil that is in our midst.

When a person opens oneself up to false teachings, these demons – or fallen angels are able to manifest in meetings at will. Many will do so because pastors and leaders have flung their doors wide open to doctrines of demons, allowing them to pollute the teachings that are going forth from the pulpit. They have invited Jezebel to come and rule and reign with them.

The apostasy will only continue to increase, with false anointings operating from false prophets and false teachers – deceiving and seducing many away from truth, with false words, signs and miracles – all lying wonders. The source of the false anointing is witchcraft – whether directly or indirectly involved in the 'craft.' [Matthew 24:24, 2 Thessalonians 2:9].

MATTHEW 7:15-16

Beware of false prophets, who come to you in sheep's clothing, but inwardly they are ravenous wolves. You will know them by their fruits. Do men gather grapes from thornbushes or figs from thistles?

The Lord forewarned us not to be deceived by them, and that we would know them by their fruit. The Church is full of wolves in sheep's clothing. The Lord wants no one to be deceived by them, but He alone is the way, the truth and the life. If we enter through any other door it will lead us into deception [John 10:1].

The false anointing draws the masses who cannot discern the real from the false. It opens the door wide open in a believer's life to the occult, if not grounded in the Word. These workers of darkness –

the witches, warlocks, wizards, who are in our midst, work overtime hexing and vexing Christians. They are causing these very real demonic influences to prey on our weaknesses, keeping many in bondage to sin – full of pride and in rebellion against the truth of the Word of God that sets us free. John spoke of this demonic influence in Revelation 16:13-14.

REVELATION 16:13-14

And I saw three unclean spirits like frogs coming out of the mouth of the dragon, out of the mouth of the beast, and out of the mouth of the false prophet. For they are spirits of demons, performing signs, which go out to the kings of the earth and of the whole world, to gather them to the battle of that great day of God Almighty.

These demonic oppressions and influences have greatly infiltrated our churches and ministry meetings, mainly operating from the spirits of Jezebel and Ashtoreth – whose root is witchcraft. It will be the main battle that the true Church – His Bride, will contend with in these last days. It is not a battle for the faint-hearted. But rather, it is for the sanctified by truth, consecrated, holy unto the Lord, purified vessels of noble use who are completely dead to self. It is for those who are making themselves ready, by sitting in the Refiner's fire until Christ has been completely conformed within them, so that they can be filled with the glory – the Seven Spirits of the Lord, and they will move in the powers of the age to come [Isaiah 11:2, Hebrews 6:5].

Eleventh Hour Laborers

For that is the answer for the onslaught of evil that we will be facing in these last days. It will be the only thing that can defeat the works of Jezebel and Ashtoreth. What Elijah failed to do – by not eliminating all the false prophets of Jezebel, we cannot afford not to do. For we are the eleventh-hour laborers – His best wine that He saved for last – for such a time as this! It is time for the Bride of Christ to arise and rebuild the broken-down walls, starting in the Sanctuary. One who will know how to labor with one hand, and wield her sword effectively in the other, until every captive that can be set free is free. Until every soul that can be saved is saved!

Best of Times and Worst of Times

It will be the worst of times, but also the best of times, for those who are willing to pay the price. Those who will deny themselves, take up their cross and follow the Lamb wherever He may lead. For those who will overcome by the blood of the Lamb, by the word of their testimony and who will not love their own life unto death – it will be the best of times [Luke 14:26-27, 33, Matthew 16:24, Rev. 12:11].

On June 13, 2020 a word of the Lord came to me while I was pondering the famous quote by Charles Dickens, *"It was the best of times and it was the worst of times."*[5] While thinking about that quote, the Holy Spirit spoke:

"It will be the best of times for those who are making themselves ready. It will be the worst of times for those who are not." AMEN!

CHAPTER 2

WE WRESTLE NOT AGAINST FLESH AND BLOOD

Finally, my brethren, be strong in the Lord and in the power of His might. Put on the whole armor of God, that you may be able to stand against the wiles of the devil. For we do not wrestle against flesh and blood, but against principalities, against powers, against the rulers of the darkness of this age, against spiritual hosts of wickedness in the heavenly places. Therefore take up the whole armor of God, that you may be able to withstand in the evil day, and having done all, to stand. Stand therefore, having girded your waist with truth, having put on the breastplate of righteousness, and having shod your feet with the preparation of the gospel of peace; above all, taking the shield of faith with which you will be able to quench all the fiery darts of the wicked one. And take the helmet of salvation, and the sword of the Spirit, which is the word of God; praying always with all prayer and supplication in the Spirit, being watchful to this end with all perseverance and supplication for all the saints [Ephesians 6:10-18].

Many Do Not Believe in Demons

There are many Christians who do not believe in demons. And yet, there are many who do believe in them, but do not believe they have any power over a child of God who has been bought and paid with the redemptive blood of the Lord Jesus. Therefore, they believe they do not need to concern themselves with this demonic activity. Those beliefs are scripturally unsound, and will cause a Christian to be snared in the demonic warfare that rages against them, leaving them without strategy in how to be free. At best, they will stay a 'lukewarm' Christian – living a carnal life full of the world – a life of compromise. Worst case, their lives may end prematurely, not fulfilling the works the Father has sent them to this earth to complete.

JAMES 4:7
Therefore submit to God. Resist the devil and he will flee from you.

1 PETER 5:8-9
Be sober, be vigilant; because your adversary the devil walks about like a roaring lion, seeking whom he may devour. Resist him, steadfast in the faith, knowing that the same sufferings are experienced by your brotherhood in the world.

A Dark, Evil Being

On June 22, 2015, I had an encounter where the Lord allowed me to have just a taste of how wicked these demons and fallen angels are, and how they come literally to kill us, if they can. After a time of worship and waiting on the Lord, I found myself battling for my life with a dark, evil being.

In the encounter, I found myself outside in front of my apartment complex. It would have been a little before my 1:00 A.M. prayer watch, when I would have taken my dog to relieve herself, before starting my time with the Lord.

I was not with my dog, but the moment I turned the corner and walked outside the gate that leads to the grass area where I would take her, everything changed! In a split second, I was knocked off my feet, and found myself in full force battle with a dark, evil being that seemed to have no form, but at the same time had a form. We were both on the ground – on our sides, facing each other. I was on my right side. This dark, evil being had such a powerful grip on me, that I was entangled and pinned to the ground by it. The only part of my body that had any movement was my left arm and left knee.

I was fighting fiercely to break free, but it was hard to get any leverage as my body was literally squashed against this evil being. It had what felt like an arm wrapped around my waist holding me down, with its other arm forcibly keeping my neck and head pinned to the ground. In its left hand that was near my head, it had a large, open safety-pin that was about 3" long. It was fiercely trying to stab the centre of my head with it. It was just known to me, if it succeeded that jab would kill me.

A great battle pursued. I thrust as hard and as often as I could, with my left knee into what would be its gut, shouting, *"Go back to hell, in the name of Jesus."* This was enough to enable me to maneuver my right hand above my head. And with my right thumb and forefinger, I was then able to grab hold of the safety-pin.

I placed my right thumb on the outside to steady it, and strategically positioned my right forefinger at the bottom of the pin, where the two sides joined. I somehow was able to apply great force to the pin this way, enabling me to keep the sharp needle point away from my head, preventing it from stabbing me. It was literally inches away from my head, but the way the Lord had me apply pressure to it, kept it away from me so it could not stab me.

Utter Darkness

This battle continued for some time. Many times, I did not think I had the strength to keep fighting. But I was finally able to wrestle the safety-pin out of this dark, evil being's hand. As I did, I commanded it to, *"Go back to hell! In the name of Jesus!"* At that point the evil being is gone. As I stand up, all I can see is darkness, but it had form to it. It was dense like fog, where you cannot see anything in front of you, but at the same time, there is brightness to the fog. In this case the darkness had the form of fog, but no brightness – I could only see utter darkness.

I was now standing near the curb of the sidewalk, facing the street. I now see the area where the battle had just taken place, was slightly raised. Not very high but like a platform. Perhaps it was a throne of darkness? As I stood there, I knew that I had secured the weapon. I then took my sword that was in my right hand, and raised it to the heavens above and declared, *"I take the sword of the Spirit in my hand, which is the Word of God, and command you go back to hell now, never to return to me again, in the name of Jesus."*

When I looked up to see my sword, I could not see it, only darkness – but knew that my sword was really long, high and piercing through that darkness. At the same time, I knew that by the blood of the Lamb and by the testimony of my words it was done. That the battle was done and won by the Lord – for the battle is truly the Lords!

As I turn around to go back into my apartment, I see that I am no longer surrounded by utter darkness. I now see the front of my apartment complex, as it would be in the natural – the dense, fog-like darkness is gone. As I walk by the grass area where I just fought this battle, I see a few small stuffed dolls and animals scattered there. I stop and pick them up and walk through the gate back into my apartment complex.

My Body Hurt

When I came out of this encounter it was close to midnight. I had no idea what I had just experienced, but I knew my body hurt. Both my hands hurt. My right hand more so than my left, and particularly my right thumb and first forefinger. My left leg and calf hurt somewhat, as well as the back of my neck – the left side more than right. My head and body ached, so much so that I took some Ibuprofen, which I normally would not take.

2 CORINTHIANS 12:2-6

I know a man in Christ who fourteen years ago —
whether in the body I do not know, or whether out of
the body I do not know, God knows — such a one was

caught up to the third heaven. And I know such a man — whether in the body or out of the body I do not know, God knows — how he was caught up into Paradise and heard inexpressible words, which it is not lawful for a man to utter. Of such a one I will boast; yet of myself I will not boast, except in my infirmities. For though I might desire to boast, I will not be a fool; for I will speak the truth...

During my time with the Lord that morning, I could only ponder this with Him – for it troubled me greatly! What did I just experience and why? Although, I had not encountered this realm before in this way, I believed He had allowed it to train me, so I can really see what is taking place in the spirit realm that fights against us, and not just head knowledge.

In the natural, it would seem almost impossible that a person could be killed with a large safety-pin, but the Holy Spirit reminded me that those who practice voodoo and witchcraft will use 'pins' to place spells and curses on their subjects of interest. They will use small stuffed dolls to represent their subject of interest. All with the evil intent of trying to manipulate and destroy people's lives.

The 'weapon' used against me was secured only because of the Lord's grace and strength. Only He could have shown me where to strategically position my right hand, thumb and forefinger on that open safety-pin, keeping the open needle away from my head during that violent struggle. And, at the same time, giving me the strength and where to place that strength – on the strongest part of safety-pin that could bear that force, enabling me to wrestle it out of the grip of that dark, evil being's hand.

ISAIAH 28:6 AMP.
And a spirit of justice to him who sits in judgment and administers the law, and strength to those who turn back the battle at the gate.

That morning before going to work, I was further shown that although the 'weapon' that had been formed against me was now secured and out of the enemy's hand, I still needed to destroy that weapon and all the curses, spells and voodoo that were associated with it, by doing a prophetic act. This act would entail taking a safety-pin, laying it on His altar and pouring the blood of the Lamb over it to destroy it. So I placed a large safety-pin on a plastic bag on the floor, and poured grape juice over it, representing the Lamb's blood. I declared that by the blood of the Lamb, no weapon formed against me, and this particular one, will prosper, and every spell, curse and all voodoo attached to this weapon has now been destroyed, never to touch my life again, in Jesus name!

The Source was Voodoo

I was still troubled by what I had encountered, yet relieved as I had been shown the source of this evil – voodoo, and believed I had now taken care of it His way. But this was not the end of the story, or my training.

While at work that day, I did not feel so great. I did not realise I had a fever until later that night. It would come and go over the next couple of days. Then a pain settled in the centre of my stomach. It was a dull pain, but caused great discomfort. The fever was gone, at least I thought, but the pain in my stomach became more persistent, spreading across the middle of my back. I could find no comfort in any position, or anything that I tried. Standing up, lying down, taking a hot bath – Ibuprofen, nothing lessened the pain. Soon the fever was back.

This went on for four days. Every day, I thought I was going to turn the corner, to find I was getting worse, much worse. On the fifth day, I knew I was in serious trouble – for I could barely walk and take care of my dog. It was rare for me to ever catch a cold, let alone anything as debilitating that I was now facing. I knew it was directly related to this horrible attack and battle that I had endured in the spirit realm.

In the wee hours I reached out to a true General in the Lord's army for counsel, whom I had known had a similar situation. They had been allowed to be attacked by the enemy for their training and would have died, if the Lord had not healed them. I shared my encounter, and the prophetic act that I had done to cleanse me from this voodoo, asking if there was anything that they could tell me to do differently, for I was rapidly declining.

I knew that I was going to die, if my physical condition did not change soon, and those would not normally be my first thoughts! I also knew it was not my time to die, for I had not completed the works that the Father has sent me to this earth to complete. So, in my debilitated state, I kept fighting to live and not die, His way and not man's way. For I knew I was not to go to a hospital, but instead I was to trust in His faithfulness to deliver and rescue that which belongs to Him.

PSALM 91-15-6

He shall call upon Me, and I will answer him; I will be with him in trouble; I will deliver and honor him. With long life I will satisfy him, and show him My salvation.

I Refuse to Die!

It was a long, dark soul night, which I spent clinging tightly to the only One Who can save me. Reminding Him of His promises, and that I refuse to die before it was my time! Not able to care for myself or my dog, and with no one near to help, a thought came to mind: to call a dear sister in the Lord, who lived two and a half hours away, and ask if she would come help me. At 4:45 A.M. I phoned to find out that she had just driven to Phoenix that night, and was only a half-mile away from me, dog-sitting! How good, kind and faithful is the Lover of our soul!

That was the beginning of my recovery. She came bearing gifts – some activated charcoal that she said the Holy Spirit told her to bring. We talked and prayed, and I took the activated charcoal. Within two hours 95% of my pain was gone. I improved greatly the rest of the day and night, but was still very weak. The next morning the Lord spoke to me. He told me that this affliction came from voodoo, from those who wanted to kill me. He allowed it to train me in this type of warfare, and that I was not to go to a doctor, as that had been a thought I had. And He told me what dose of activated charcoal that I was to take instead.

I still did not understand why I had become so sick in the first place, as I was able to stop that dark, evil being from piercing my head with the safety-pin. I had broken their magic off my life fairly quickly. I wanted to know what I did wrong or missed? What I understood from the Lord was that the reason that I got so sick was because every place that dark, evil being had forcibly pinned my body to the ground, its evil poison was able to enter my physical body. It is why the different parts of my body hurt – they were held by that powerful evil grip. I understood that I would have died, if that pin had pierced my head; that if I had not done the things I was shown to do – the prophetic act destroying the 'weapon' with the blood of the Lamb, therefore destroying the voodoo off my life, and having the blood of the Lamb cleanse me of it – it would have been worse. I understood that my sickness was the residual effects of being in battle – a battle scar so to speak, for death was their goal.

For about a week, I suffered a new ailment every day. One day my legs would be weak and I thought they would buckle beneath me. That would go away and then it would be chest pain, or something else. My taste buds changed and I could no longer drink coffee – it was unappealing to me. If the Lord had not told me not to go to a doctor, I would have gone to one. But He was growing my faith to believe He is my Healer, an area of my faith that needed to be strengthened. It took a few months before I was completely recovered, but the Lord was faithful to heal me in every way.

When I did hear back from the person that I had reached out to for counsel, this is what they wrote:

*"Tracy, you certainly were in battle for real. The demons have now come down to the earth in unprecedented levels, so you may not have been in the 2nd heaven, but in the earth's night watches, when witchcraft is the most powerful. My recent battle was also very real, and allowed by YHVH, so that I would acquire more endurance and learn to press in against great pressure and demonic power. Our bodies can get injured in the battle, but during our healing time the Lord teaches us trust without fear, and to inquire of Him, in regard to what healing steps to take (sometimes it is going to a MD). You made the correct connection with the voodoo attack and the pin. You dispatched the threat very well. A suggestion I would give you, **is that you must command the demon to depart in the name, blood, and authority of Yeshua Ha Mashiach.** In the name of Jesus, without stating His title and authority, is very weak. It also helps a great deal to state who you are. You are a blood-bought, redeemed daughter of the Most High God, a bond servant, who lives under His protection, authority and leadership."*

Different Classes of Evil Spirits

In this encounter, I had been allowed to experience some of the dark powers that operate in the heavenlies. I believe I wrestled with a fallen angel and not a demon. Demons and fallen angels are different classes of evil spirits, with different powers and authority assigned to them. Demons are disembodied, unclean spirits that are sent to influence a person's soul. We see an example of this when Jesus arrived in Gadarenes and encountered the two men under the control of demons. Those demons begged the Lord to send them into the pigs, who then committed a mass pig suicide.

Because of it, the people grew fearful and begged the Lord to depart from their town. Have you ever wondered why the people begged the Lord to depart? You would think, after witnessing what

He did, they would have begged Him to stay! These scriptures show the 'influence' of principalities. Principalities rule over regions and they influence people's souls to do evil. Different regions have different principalities over them, which are directly related to the predominate sin in that city or region. It is why the people begged the Lord to depart. There were demons operating under that ruling principality who influenced the people, causing them to be deluded and deceived. They could not see the good the Lord brought to them [Matthew 8:28-34].

Fallen angels have bodily form, and they too influence people's soul to do evil, but they have more power and authority than unclean, disembodied spirits. Lucifer would be a fallen angel. And when he rebelled against God and was cast out of heaven, he caused an unholy revolt to take place and caused a third of the angels to fall with him. And those angels that fell with him still have access to our lives today to do Satan's evil works [Luke 10:18, Revelation 12:4, 7-9, 2 Peter 2:4].

LUKE 10:18
And He said to them, "I saw Satan fall like lightning from heaven.

REVELATION 12:7-9
And war broke out in heaven: Michael and his angels fought with the dragon; and the dragon and his angels fought, but they did not prevail, nor was a place found for them in heaven any longer. So the great dragon was cast out, that serpent of old, called the Devil and Satan, who deceives the whole world; he was cast to the earth, and his angels were cast out with him.

2 PETER 2:4
For if God did not spare the angels who sinned, but cast them down to hell and delivered them into chains of darkness, to be reserved for judgment.

No Option but to Fight!

When I was in that fierce battle for my life, despite the times I thought I could no longer resist that dark, evil being, I had absolutely no fear! There was no option but to fight, and to fight like my life depended upon it, because it did! Our battles are either won or lost in prayer. We need strategy – heaven's counsel to guide our every move. For there are times we will wrestle with the demonic realm. Paul said that we wrestle not with flesh and blood – he meant what he said! It is a real wrestling with demonic beings, not some figure of speech.

Most in the Church are not aware of this wrestling with demonic beings, because their spiritual eyes have not been opened. But they feel their devastating affect in their lives. As believers, we need to know that the spirit realm is more real than the natural realm. That there are real demons and fallen angels that are sent into our lives to destroy us, and the source of their power is mainly fueled by witchcraft. I believe if more believers experienced it in the way I was allowed, it would surely cause most to flee from that place of complacency. AMEN!

CHAPTER 3

SIGN OF THE TIMES

He answered and said to them, "When it is evening you say, 'It will be fair weather, for the sky is red'; and in the morning, 'It will be foul weather today, for the sky is red and threatening.' Hypocrites! You know how to discern the face of the sky, but you cannot discern the signs of the times [Matthew 16:2-3].

Beloved, we are in the last days – the Lord Jesus' Second Coming and return is much sooner than most believe! There is a spiritual war raging in our nations in this hour as never before seen. That war is raging against all of mankind, trying to stop the Lamb from receiving the reward of His suffering, in the fullest measure, which is for the nations to be saved [Psalm 2:8].

Nations are made up of people. And that war is raging in the second heavens, trying to stop people, tribes, tongues and nations from fulfilling their destinies. There is a war raging against the true Church – the Bride of Christ, all trying to stop revival from coming. Trying to stop the Lord of the Harvest from receiving His harvest in due season.

The Lord desires us to be like the Sons of Issachar who will know the times and seasons of God. He is looking for a people to make a habitation with – vessels who have made themselves ready, which Revelation 19:7 and 2 Chronicles 16:9 speak about.

REVELATION 19:7 AMP.
Let us rejoice and shout for joy [exulting and triumphant]! Let us celebrate and ascribe to Him glory and honor, for

*the marriage of the Lamb has come, and His bride has
prepared herself.*

2 Chronicles 16:9 AMP.
*For the eyes of the Lord run to and fro throughout the
whole earth to show Himself strong in behalf of those
whose hearts are blameless toward Him.*

They are those vessels who will receive the end result of their
faith, the salvation of their soul. This should be our number one
priority as a believer in the Lord Jesus, until Christ is completely
conformed within us [1 Peter 1:9, Galatians 4:19]. I repeat this so
often. Why? Because it is the Lord's answer for the dark days that
we will be facing, not only to endure them, but to persevere and
overcome them, His way [Revelation 3:10, 21].

Stand Against the Wiles of the Devil

In Ephesians 6:11,13 Paul exhorts us to put on the whole armor
of God, that we would be able to stand against the wiles of the devil
– to stand against his strategies and deceit. That we would be able
to stand in the evil day. In both verses, Paul tells us to put on the full
armor of God, not a partial covering. This is vital if we are to overcome
the strategies of the enemy that are constantly raging against us.

Ephesians 6:11, 13
*Put on the whole armor of God, that you may be able
to stand against the wiles of the devil. Therefore take
up the whole armor of God, that you may be able to
withstand in the evil day, and having done all, to stand.*

Any good soldier engaged in a military battle would not do so
without covering themselves head to foot in protective gear – helmet,
bullet proof vests, camouflage clothing and protective combat boots,
with their weapons of warfare buckled securely around their waist.

Equally, they make sure all their weapons are working properly. That they are cleaned and oiled after every use, prepared to engage in the next combative assault. They do not assume how long the battle will last; therefore, they carry extra ammunition to not be caught off guard. They would know their rank and file and would not usurp authority – avoiding 'friendly fire' at all cost!

The Lord is looking for His people to be prepared not just spiritually, but physically, emotionally, and financially for those who are called to be 'Josephs' who will have storehouses to provide for those in need. These will be needed for when the banking and retail industries no longer operate, as we have known. Also, these will be important when the nations move into cashless societies, and when our only means to buy and sell will be, if one has taken the Mark of the Beast [Revelation 13:16-17].

REVELATION 13:16-17

He causes all, both small and great, rich and poor, free and slave, to receive a mark on their right hand or on their foreheads, and that no one may buy or sell except one who has the mark or the name of the beast, or the number of his name.

As Christians, we cannot stay passive, deceived in a comfortable place of complacency. We have a real call to action on our part. We are not going to be able to stand the evil day, if we are not preparing in all of these areas in our lives, in an intimate, love relationship where Jesus is Lord over all. Standing the evil day is going to take more than hiding out in our prayer closets – but that is an excellent place to start! A mature prayer life is vital to completing the eternal purposes of God in our lives. It is heaven's love language. It is how our Creator chose to communicate with us. It is how and where we get strategies to move forward in the plans of God for our personal lives, churches and ministries. It is where the battles we face, whether in our personal lives or in our nations, are either won or lost.

Prayer is a call to action from our Creator to co-partner with Him to bring about His eternal plans on earth as they exist in heaven. It requires our response. If we have a hit and miss prayer life – and not living a holy, consecrated life unto the Lord, we more than likely are losing many battles that we did not need to lose.

The Choice Will Be Ours

The choice will be ours. Do we want to stay a lukewarm Christian that Revelation 3:16 says the Lord will vomit out? We become lukewarm by walking in compromise. By wanting to please man, and not the Lord. By following the doctrines of demons that have infiltrated the Church, with false grace teachings that have put most in a slumber. Do we want to hold onto the doctrine of man that says we are not going through the tribulation? This teaching that wants to convince us that we do not need to be concerned about the Mark of the Beast? If we do, then we are not going to be prepared for the days that are only getting darker.

Or, better yet, do we want to be 100% sold-out, on fire for the Lord Jesus? Vessels who will overcome by the blood of the Lamb, by the word of our testimony, and not loving our lives unto death? Most in the Church have been lulled into a slumber by believing doctrines of demons. They have been deceived to believe what their itching ears want to hear. Seduced and flattered to believe what makes their flesh feel good. To believe "Peace, peace, when there is no peace." How can anyone say there is peace on this earth when we look all around and see the nations being tossed to and fro? Tossed to and fro, not only with the judgments of the Lord that are being released, but equally by the evil schemes of wicked ones that dwell on earth, who have one purpose: to destroy the plans of God for mankind, at the cost of their soul being destroyed.

The Lord forewarns in Matthew 24:22-23 that if those days had not been shortened no one would survive, but for the sake of the elect those days have been shortened. That even the very elect can be deceived. What days was the Lord talking about? The evil day that Paul spoke about in Ephesians 6:13 – the last days that we are living in.

Robots and Plagues

In early 2017, the European Parliament reported that they want to adopt a 'Robot Bill of Rights.'[6] Since then we have seen drones enforce cities. With the 2020 riots in the USA, and the globalists' call to defund the police, we are seeing the call for robots to replace police officers. It is an evil scheme of Satan – wanting to replace mankind with robots. By doing so, if he succeeded, it would be his ultimate insult to Creator God, for man was created in God's image. Satan despises that fact and has been working ever since the fall of man to destroy God's image that is imprinted upon every person's soul when they are born into this world.

In January and February 2020, we saw the Coronavirus Pandemic breakout in the nations. Dr. Judy Mikovits, a world-renowned molecular scientist in immunology and virology, along with Kent Heckenlively, a former attorney, wrote a book called *Plague of Corruption*.[7] The book reveals what has been taking place in the vaccine world. And because of her book, many refer to Covid-19 as 'the plague of corruption.'

We have seen our nations go into lockdown, implementing martial law – house arrest, all under the guise of our health and safety. Governments and mainstream media have pushed this evil, globalists' agenda creating fear and panic, by governments skewing the death statistics with the media reporting them daily. Many deaths have been recorded to have died with Covid-19, when they actually died from other illnesses.

We have seen mandatory laws sprout up overnight telling us how to protect ourselves from this virus. That we need to implement social distancing, face masks, handwashing and isolation to name a few. But what most are not aware of though, is that there is an evil agenda behind these orders that 'seem' to be for our good. They are occultic rituals designed by the Luciferians to try to strip us of our identity in Christ.

In the natural they seem to be good and God does want us to be healthy. The Bible has examples of how He deals with diseases; the lepers were to isolate themselves. So we can see some parallels.

But the difference is that those were God's holy ways to deal with disease with the lepers, and they applied to the sick only – not to the healthy. They were His way to heal and restore us. Whereas, the source of these current mandates is not from God, but is coming from globalists, who want to control and destroy us. Isolating both the sick and the well. These mandates are not designed to keep us well, but are actually designed to 'spiritually' control and destroy us.

They are trying to manipulate us so that we would take on the new world order's identity. Steve Barwick wrote an in-depth article entitled: *Occult Ritual Transformation and Coronavirus: How Mask Wearing, Hand Washing, Social Separation and Lockdowns Are Age-Old Occult Rituals Being Used to Initiate People into a New Global Order.*[8] He explains these rituals, that I pray will be an eye opener to help us to be aware of the evil schemes and to know how to pray against them.

These rituals are a pre-conditioning that want to bewitch and beguile us, by persuasive arguments and beguiling speech that have come forth from governments, the World Health Organization, the United Nations and from other globalists' organisations who are promoting mandatory vaccines.

But we do not need to fear their occultic rituals, for our God is greater! If He is for us – who can be against us! We can defeat this evil with prayer, by applying the blood of the Lamb to the root of these occultic rituals and command their evil counsel against our lives, cities and nations to be destroyed in the name of the Lord Jesus Christ! Amen!

So why are they doing all of this? There are many reasons, but I believe the biggest one is to push for a mandatory vaccine, saying it will be our only cure. It will be 'praised' as a way to stop the spread of this virus, while giving people back their 'freedom' for those who will take it. But it will come at a price that most have no idea they are being asked to pay – eventually the cost of their soul. Beloved, beware! The vaccine will be a conduit, setting up the nations to receive the Mark of the Beast.

This is only the beginning of the evil day that we are to stand against! The shakings are here. It will be much more wicked in the days to come. There will be more global plagues coming. Some will be man-made, while others will be the judgments of God. But as His praying remnant, the Lord does not want us troubled, but to keep watch in prayer. We do not need to fear the evil schemes, but to be aware of them, and be prepared. To be prepared is to be armed.

Remember that when the plague broke out in the Israelite's camp, Moses sent Aaron into their midst with the censer and the plague stopped. Many lost their lives, but the point I want to highlight is that the Lord is looking to us, His Ekklesia, to be His antidote to the plagues, whether they are man-made or from God. He does not want us to be fearful. He wants us prepared to respond to Him in a way that will draw others unto Him.

NUMBERS 16:46-48

So Moses said to Aaron, "Take a censer and put fire in it from the altar, put incense on it, and take it quickly to the congregation and make atonement for them; for wrath has gone out from the Lord. The plague has begun. "Then Aaron took it as Moses commanded, and ran into the midst of the assembly; and already the plague had begun among the people. So he put in the incense and made atonement for the people. And he stood between the dead and the living; so the plague was stopped.

The Coronavirus was a test run for the Church, albeit devised by evil hearts. But the Lord has allowed it for our good, wanting us to be prepared for these dark days. He is shaking all that can be shaken, so that the only thing which will remain, will be that which cannot be shaken – truth. For there are much greater shakings that are yet to come.

HEBREWS 12:26-27

...but now He has promised, saying, "Yet once more I shake not only the earth, but also heaven. "Now this,

*"Yet once more," indicates the removal of those things
that are being shaken, as of things that are made, that
the things which cannot be shaken may remain.*

The Mark of the Beast is about to Arrive!

The Mark of the Beast is about to arrive publicly! The European Union – Brussels and Strasburg, the W.H.O. along with the Vatican are working together, using technology and health to bring about their new world order and a one world religion.

Pope Francis and the Vatican have been advocating a one-world religion for years. The Pope openly states that we need to have diversity of religions, and he made a covenant – an unholy alliance with Islam, when he signed the *Document of Human Fraternity* with the Grand Iman of Al-Azhar Ahmad Al-Tayyeb, in Abu Dhabi on February 4, 2019.[9]

Pope Francis's teachings are biblically unsound. He is on the record for denying that hell exists.[10] At a youth meeting in the United States, he told those attending that Christians should not proselytize.[11] Equally disturbing, a Vatican Emissary Cardinal had dined with a high-ranking witch during the Davos 2018 meetings.[12] Pope Francis is one to keep our eyes on.

On August 2, 2017, a Wisconsin company in the United States, Three Square Market, was the first American company to chip their employees. It was on a voluntary basis, and 41 of their 85 employees received a microchip implant in their hand.[13] As of October 22, 2018 more than 4,000 Swedes have been microchipped.[14]

In the beginning of 2020, we saw new terminology sprout up overnight from our governments: contact tracing, social distancing, self-isolate, new normal. And we have seen how Google and Apple have worked with them to implement an App to be downloaded onto our phones.[15] The so-called purpose of this App is to track people who have come into contact with others who have this virus. All under the guise of our well-being, to prevent the spread of this virus. This trap and snare has been laid with the goal to control the people, and lead the masses like sheep to the slaughter to take the Mark of the Beast.

Beloved, if we are anything less than 100% sold-out for the Lord, by denying our will in exchange for His in every area of our lives, we will be deceived in these last days. We will walk after the flesh as an enemy to God, for our carnal mind is death, and our flesh cannot please Him. We will make decisions based on our fleshly desires, fear, or the popular view of the hour, and not make decisions based on truth. We will not walk after the Spirit. Instead, we will end up being swept away in a flood of destruction, for the coming of the Son of Man will be like it was in the days of Noah, if we choose not to be prepared [Romans 8:1, 6-8, Matthew 24:37-39].

Born into The Kingdom for Such a Time as This!

So how should we respond? Do we bury our heads in the sand, and become fearful and take no responsibility by staying silent on the sidelines? Esther tried to do that, until her cousin Mordechai rebuked her, jolting her out of her complacency. He told her that if she stayed silent, she and her father's house would perish. He reminded her that she had come into the kingdom for such a time as this [Esther 4:14].

I believe we can learn a lot from Nehemiah, as well. He was born into captivity and lived in Shushan as the king's cupbearer. Nehemiah is a book of restoration. A restoration of the remnant who survived the exile. God restored them from utter ruins and turned them back to righteousness and the eternal plans of God for them as a people, tribe, tongue and nation.

We see with Nehemiah, that one man's sacrificial, humble prayers, fasting and tears, while in Babylon, moved the heart of God to use him mightily to restore his people back to truth, purity, holiness and the fear of the Lord. He restored them back to God's commandments without compromise, where they worshipped in spirit and in truth.

Nehemiah was fearless and he did not walk in compromise. He confronted sin and the issues of his day, head on. He was faithful, focused and committed. There was nothing that was going to distract, or take him away from the assignment at hand, which was rebuilding the broken-down walls of his beloved city, Jerusalem.

He knew God intimately, and therefore, he had no fear of man manipulating the decisions he made. It is one of the reasons that God could use him so mightily to bring restoration to a broken people. At the same time, Nehemiah was a warrior – he had strategy in battle!

Fearlessness Caused the Early Church to Grow

It was primarily fearlessness – no fear of man, that caused the early Church to grow. The established leadership was offended often by the Apostles' bold stand for their preaching of Jesus – the unadulterated, pure teachings of Christ.

1 THESSALONIANS 2:4
But as we have been approved by God to be entrusted with the gospel, even so we speak, not as pleasing men, but God who tests our hearts.

When Peter and John were thrown in prison for healing the crippled man at the gate called Beautiful and for teaching the people about Jesus, the Pharisaical leadership told them not to ever preach the name Jesus again. They refused to obey man and instead obeyed God, no matter what the cost. When they were released from prison, they prayed for the Lord to grant them full freedom to fearlessly preach the Word. Because they did, a great movement of the Holy Spirit came and filled them while they assembled and prayed, causing thousands to follow Jesus. [Acts 3:1-6, 4:1-2, 19, 29-31].

ACTS 4:29-31
Now, Lord, look on their threats, and grant to Your servants that with all boldness they may speak Your word, by stretching out Your hand to heal, and that signs and wonders may be done through the name of Your holy Servant Jesus." And when they had prayed, the

place where they were assembled together was shaken; and they were all filled with the Holy Spirit, and they spoke the word of God with boldness.

Today, we have many churches that may have several thousand members and adding to them every week. But are they growing in the knowledge of the Lord? Are they being conformed into His likeness – in their words, thought life and deeds? Are people's lives having lasting good fruit coming forth? Is transformation *'Zoe'* life taking place?

Most pastors and leaders are not teaching Christ crucified, and what it means to be a true disciple of Christ [Luke 14:26-27, 33]. They may grow in members, but they will not grow in the character of Christ. They will miss the eternal purposes for which we were created. We all have Kingdom assignments to complete on earth, and these assignments are meant to mold and shape us into His image – into His divine Character. This transformation will cause us to be equally yoked with Him, and to become the Bride of Christ. This can only take place if we are willing to deny ourselves and exchange our will for His.

Bridal and War Preparation

At large, the Church is asleep with very few in bridal preparation – meaning, sitting in the Refiner's fire until every spot and wrinkle has been removed from our soul. Equally, most are not in war preparation either, for they are not taught how to be a warrior for Christ. It is a battle that we are all in, whether we know it or not. Yet, we have so few believers engaging in the battle on a governmental level.

We are facing life and death issues in the nations, as we have not seen in decades. The Lord is looking to His Church to stand against the evil that is in our midst. As His Ekklesia – He expects us to! *'Ekklesia'* is the Greek word for 'church' in the New Testament. It means, 'called-out ones' or 'a governing body of people.' 'Church' is not the best translation of *'ekklesia.'* It tends to make us think of a building where we gather, instead of a company of people who are to execute His righteousness on this earth.

If we are to effectively engage in the battle, we need to understand what it means to be His 'Church.' We are not called to be a 'church' built by man's hands, but a church – or *ekklesia*, that has not been built by man's hands. We are not called to be formed into man's image, but into His. We are to be a company of people who will execute righteousness on this earth. The Lord holds His Church accountable for the state of affairs not only in the Church, but in our nation's governments. We see this with the parable of the talents [Luke 19:11-27].

Passion Attracts the Lord

So, how can we be a church not built by man's hands? If we have passion for the Lord it will cause His plans to manifest in our lives. For passion attracts the Lord. We see this with Zacchaeus in Luke 19. Although he was small in stature, he ran ahead and climbed a sycamore tree so he could see the Lord, for he had to see Him with his own eyes! Because of it, it got the Lord's attention. When He passed by, He told Zacchaeus to hurry up and come down – that He must stay at his house today! Zacchaeus's passion caused him to have a personal, intimate encounter with the Lover of His soul. We might ask ourselves then, are we like Zacchaeus, passionately following the Lord, not caring what man thinks?

Have we accepted the Bride's invite, that the Lord spoke about in the wedding banquet parable in Matthew 22? Are we prepared? Do we have on the right garments to attend that wedding banquet – ones that are without spot or wrinkle? Are we the five wise virgins filling our lamps with oil? That speaks of an intimate relationship with Him. Are we dying to self so that we can be filled with His glory? Or, are we the five foolish virgins, consumed in our own selfish desires and pursuits, thinking we can have one foot in this world and one foot in His Kingdom [Matthew 22:1-14, 25:1-10, Ephesians 5:27]?

The Lord is pure and holy. He not only desires, but requires us to be holy as He is holy. He is not going to marry a harlot. But a Bride who is 100% on fire for Him. One who is passionately head over heels in love with Him, who has no other lovers. One who has only one agenda to know Him and to do His will, no matter what it may cost her [Philippians 3:8-10].

When preparing for a meeting in March 2018, there was a news article that came out, reporting how a wedding gown shop in Dublin, Ireland, overnight closed their doors without any warning, leaving 200 brides without dresses for their wedding day. There was no recourse for these women, and some had already paid a 50% deposit!

I saw this as a prophetic warning to the Church for how late the hour is, and how unprepared the Bride of Christ is for His soon Second Coming and return. A warning that her lamp is not filled with oil, and that overnight the door to the wedding supper will be shut with no recourse to enter – a picture of the five foolish virgins. As I pondered this before the Lord, a few days later on March 26, 2018 the word of the Lord came to me saying, *"Prepare My people, I AM coming soon, and My Bride has not made herself ready."*

Access, Provision and Protection

We see with Nehemiah that his heart broke for what broke the Lord's heart. He saw his people being destroyed. It was not the heart of God for them to be in utter ruins without hope. He is a God of redemption and restoration. But not to bring restoration so they could keep doing things their way – but to restore them back to the ways of God. A restoration that meant turning back to the One and True Living God in repentance for not following His ways. Nehemiah carried this counsel of God in his heart. It was the roadmap to bring hope and restoration to a broken people that desperately needed to be saved, healed and restored.

God's favor came upon him because he carried the burden of the Lord for the people to be restored to right relationship with Him. Because of it, King Artaxerxes gave Nehemiah the access – the letters he needed to pass through Euphrates into Judah. The provision – all the timber that was needed to rebuild. And protection – a military escort, that he needed to be able to rebuild the broken-down walls of his people in Jerusalem [Nehemiah 2:5,7-9].

We can find great hope and encouragement in this! As it was for Nehemiah, so too will it be for those who are making themselves ready. Those who have been sitting in the Refiner's fire for years, dying a thousand deaths, until there is only one agenda, and it is all Him. Those who no longer care about their reputation, but only His being high and lifted up. Those who only care that the desires of His high, lofty and noble heart are satisfied. For their soul yearns and aches to see His redemptive plans manifest on earth as they are in heaven, not only in their own lives, but in the nations. For they have one purpose and that is to know Him, and to complete the works the Father has sent them to this earth to complete. For the Father and Son to be glorified in and through them, by bringing forth abundant and everlasting fruit [John 17:4, 15:8, 16].

JOHN 17:4

I have glorified You on the earth. I have finished the work which You have given Me to do.

It is a positioning in Him, where we come to that place where we have to be in the centre of the Father's perfect will for our lives. No matter how uncomfortable, inconvenient or what it may cost us. It does not mean we have got it all perfect and right just yet, as we surely do not, and will keep making mistakes. But it means He has our 'yes.' That there are no other lovers but Him. No other distractions. No more compromise. That we are pursuing Him passionately out of lovesick obedience to Him – from a position of relationship, and not out of a duty of religion.

When we do, that passion that burns within our soul for those things that break His heart, will cause the favor of the Lord to come upon us. He will be faithful to provide every access, provision and protection that we need, in its appointed season. For we surely need all of them, in these last days as never before! He is the same yesterday, today and forever! He will be faithful to protect and provide for those who belong to Him. Those who have proven it by their unwavering faithfulness to know Him and to follow Him – despite their failures and flaws along the way. AMEN!

CHAPTER 4

SPIRITS OF SANBALLAT AND TOBIAH

When Sanballat the Horonite and Tobiah the servant, the Ammonite, heard this, it distressed them exceedingly that a man had come to inquire for and require the good and prosperity of the Israelites [Nehemiah 2:10].

Sanballat and Tobiah – The War Begins!

So, just like it was for Nehemiah when rebuilding the broken-down walls, he faced great warfare – so too will it be for us. Satan hates when God can find a vessel who is empty of self, and 100% yielded to the will of the Lord. The enemy tries every way possible to destroy those vessels, and the plans of God for their lives, families, cities and nation.

We see in Nehemiah that Sanballat the Horonite and Tobiah his servant, who was an Ammonite, were greatly distressed that a man had come requiring the good of his people [Nehemiah 2:10, 19]. Nehemiah was Sanballat's and Tobiah's worst fear come true, for nothing they could do prevailed against him. Nehemiah depicts a company of people who are known as the Bride of Christ, the Overcomers – the Sons of God, who will have the full stature of Christ formed within them. They will be fearless and fearsome. They will be faithful, focused and committed. For nothing will cause them to take their eyes off the Lord's plans for them!

Because of Nehemiah's great threat to Sanballat and Tobiah, he had enemies and engaged in constant warfare against them, putting to flight their counsel against him, every time! So too, are we facing the same constant warfare with these spirits, known as Sanballat and Tobiah, when we are building according to the Lord's plans.

These spirits are very much alive and operating today in the Church, and they take their orders from Jezebel, who is their wicked task-master. They come to destroy our relationship with the Lord, and our times of prayer. They come to destroy the access, provision and protection that we need to build God's plans. They come to destroy the eternal relationships that the Lord has brought into our lives, if possible.

What are Their War Plans?

1. They come to mock us. They are angry, rageful and hateful towards us for wanting to rebuild the broken-down walls in God's way, in our relationships, in our churches and ministries and in our nations. We saw this with Nehemiah. They scorned, despised and raged against him, before he had even begun to build. They came against him strongly because he came for the good of his people. They were trying to stop him before he could even begin [Nehemiah 2:19, 4:1 AMP.].

> **NEHEMIAH 2:19 AMP.**
> *But when Sanballat the Horonite and Tobiah the servant, the Ammonite, and Geshem the Arab heard of it, they laughed us to scorn and despised us and said, what is this thing you are doing? Will you rebel against the king?*

2. They devise evil schemes against us. They send 'foxes' to break down God's plans, when we are in the process of building the Lord's way. Foxes can be many things: offenses, jealousy, rejection, competition, people or situations that are unholy alliances – adultery, pornography. Spiritual foxes search out the weakest and most vulnerable area in our hearts, and work at it until they have broken through with their agenda. We saw this with Tobiah, where he thought if they sent some foxes into Nehemiah's plans, they would be able to find the weak area and tear down the wall that they had begun to build [Nehemiah 4:3 AMP.].

NEHEMIAH 4:3 AMP.

Now Tobiah the Ammonite was near him, and he said, what they build — if a fox climbs upon it, he will break down their stone wall.

3. They come to destroy, confuse and divide. They become more aggressive in their warfare against us, when they see the laborers have begun to unite and build. They see we are serious about rebuilding His Kingdom His way, and that we are making progress – the wall is half-built, so to speak! So they come with evil plans to do us bodily harm with sicknesses, accidents or premature deaths. To cause offenses in our hearts towards one another, bringing division and confusion. They come to speak failure into our plans because they see we are united in spirit and in truth and have one agenda – the Lord's agenda [Nehemiah 4:8 AMP].

NEHEMIAH 4:8 AMP.

And they all plotted together to come and fight against Jerusalem, to injure and cause confusion and failure in it.

4. They come to weary and kill with the goal to stop God's plans. They become even more aggressive, but with a different approach, when they see their other efforts have not been successful. They come to attack the burden bearers – those who carry the Lord's burdens in that place of intercessory prayer. To attack the intercessors who are faithful to keep watch praying, until His Kingdom comes, and the Father's will is done in and through them [Luke 18:1].

LUKE 18:1

Then He spoke a parable to them, that men always ought to pray and not lose heart.

If we are to be the Bride of Christ, we will be an intercessor, regardless of the specific call that is on our lives. For it is in that place of intimacy and intercessory prayer that the plans of heaven are revealed to His Bride, giving her the strategies and blueprints that she needs to build the Kingdom of God on earth as it is in heaven. It is intercessory prayer that will cause the nations to be saved, for it is what births and fuels revival.

So, it does not matter if we are an apostle, prophet, evangelist, pastor, teacher, worship leader, youth pastor – whatever our call is, if we are to be the Bride of Christ and used mightily by the Lord in these last days, we will be an intercessor. It is where we receive the plans that will establish and direct our church or ministry's steps. Can we begin to see why the battle is so great trying to stop us from building?

So, these spirits come to weary us any way they can. To weary our minds and emotions by causing unnecessary activity or situations in our lives that take their toll on us physically, emotionally and financially, all with the goal to weaken our prayer life. For it is in that place of prayer, that intimacy and a love relationship with our Bridegroom King Jesus is developed, matured and maintained.

So, they come to kill. Physically, emotionally and financially, for they know if they do, it will stop God's plans from being complete in our lives. We are in serious warfare! It is why we are to stay vigilant in prayer, keeping watch for the thief that wants to break into our lives, to destroy and kill us [Nehemiah 4:10-11, Matthew 24:43].

NEHEMIAH 4:8, 10-11 AMP.
But because of them we made our prayer to our God and set a watch against them day and night. And [the leaders of] Judah said, the strength of the burden bearers is weakening, and there is much rubbish; we are not able to work on the wall. And our enemies said, they will not know or see till we come into their midst and kill them and stop the work.

5. They come to seduce, distract and to do us harm. If it does not work for these spirits to stop us by threatening, wearying or killing us, they try another tactic. They come to seduce us away from our Kingdom assignments and that place of prayer, with distracting interruptions. Every time we go to prayer, we are in a battle. Every time we go to pray for the Church, or for an issue in our government, or a loved one, we are in a battle! How often does the phone ring with someone wanting our time, or what seems like an emergency comes up, demanding our attention, right before we are about to pray?

The Lord tells us that the Kingdom of heaven suffers violence and that we are to take it by force [Matthew 11:12]. We have to learn to discern those seducing distractions that sometimes can appeal to our weak flesh, and we must learn to say no and not feel condemned or shamed for doing so. For those are tactics of the evil one to manipulate our emotions, taking our thoughts and time away from prayer. There is only one way to build the Kingdom of God, and it is through living a consecrated holy lifestyle, saturated with the Word and prayer – it is our only hope.

EPHESIANS 6:18-19

Praying always with all prayer and supplication in the Spirit, being watchful to this end with all perseverance and supplication for all the saints — and for me, that utterance may be given to me, that I may open my mouth boldly to make known the mystery of the gospel.

Nehemiah recognised their seduction and distractions, knowing they wanted to harm him. How did he know? He had the gift of discernment of spirits, and therefore, he did not fall for their bait. Instead, he sent a message back saying, *"I am doing a great work and cannot come down. Why should the work stop while I leave to come see you?"*

Nehemiah was faithful, focused and committed. So too will the Bride of Christ be in these last days. There will be nothing that will cause her to take her eyes off her Commander-In-Chief. Which in turn, will only cause the enemy to rage against her even more forcibly trying to destroy her [Nehemiah 6:1-3].

NEHEMIAH 6:2 AMP.

Sanballat and Geshem sent to me, saying, come, let us meet together in one of the villages in the plain of Ono. But they intended to do me harm.

6. These wicked spirits come to slander and gossip. When all their other evil tactics fail to take us out physically, they ramp it up a notch and come with a false report. They come with slander and gossip, trying to control and manipulate us with fear, so that others will believe their lies. They falsely accuse us before our families, and other church members – whatever our sphere of influence may be, they try to discredit us. They try to manipulate us into compromising the Word of God, and the plans He has for us, by giving into their counsel.

Their target – all laborers! But especially the true leadership, who are responsible for leading, guiding and implementing the plans of God. Those who are 100% sold-out to the Lord, who refuse to walk in compromise, or fear of man. We saw this with Nehemiah, when he was publicly, falsely accused of planning a revolt, accusing him of wanting to be the king of Judah.

These spirits' goal is to slander the leadership with the spirit of accusation of the brethren, to divide and conquer the laborers, and to stop God's plans in its tracks [Nehemiah 6:6-7]. But because Nehemiah was righteous before God and before man – above reproach, he was able to refute and confront their lies to their face, causing their plans against him to fail.

NEHEMIAH 6:6-7 AMP.

In it was written: It is reported among the neighboring nations, and Gashmu says it, that you and the Jews plan to rebel; therefore you are building the wall, that you may be their king, according to the report. Also you have set up prophets to announce concerning you in Jerusalem, There is a king in Judah. And now this will be reported to the [Persian] king. So, come now and let us take counsel together.

7. They come to paralyse with fear in our weakness. It is one thing to be physically attacked – that is hard! But when we get attacked in our emotions, because of false accusations and slander, it often is harder to overcome that emotional duress. These attacks tend to come when we are weary and have been laboring for some time – for years. We have made progress in the building of God's plans, with eternal relationships established along the way. We are getting closer to the highest place on the face of the earth, which is at the feet of Jesus. Meaning, we have made a lot of mistakes – many failures with great humblings that have caused our flesh to peel away and die. All milestones marking the road to perfection.

Often the journey has been painful and lonely. True leadership is marked with these battle scars. When these evil spirits think we are tired, weak and vulnerable they come trying to put fear into our minds with their lies and accusations from others. Thinking they will finally be able to stop us – that we will give up and quit. But I love Nehemiah's response! Instead, he calls for his hands to be strengthened to endure to the end – amen!

May that too be our response in the difficult, pressed-down places that we walk through, or sometimes it feels like we crawl through, remembering that He is a God of hope and encouragement. We remember that He does not want us to lose heart, to grow weary or to faint. Instead His power is brought to perfection in our weaknesses. That He gives power to the faint and weary, and to him who has no might, He increases strength [Nehemiah 6:9, Romans 15:13, Galatians 6:9, 2 Corinthians 12:9, Isaiah 40:29].

NEHEMIAH 6:9 AMP.
*For they all wanted to frighten us, thinking, their hands
will be so weak that the work will not be done. But now
strengthen my hands!*

8. They come to deceive with false prophets and teachers.
With the goal to get us to walk in fear of man, compromise and
mixture. For that is the main goal of the false prophets and teachers.
Most are so deceived they believe they are walking in truth. It is
because at one point they crossed a line by walking in compromise,
where they rejected truth one too many times. Therefore, they have
given the spirit of deception the legal right to operate in their lives.
Not only are they deceived, but they pursue those in their sphere of
influence with false words and teachings. Sadly, they are entrapping
many who are not grounded in the Word, in prayer and in an intimate,
love relationship with the Lord Jesus.

We see that the spirit of deception operates with the spirit of
Sanballat and Tobiah. A false prophet, by the name of Shemiah, lied
to Nehemiah, saying they were coming to kill him, wanting to put fear
into him. Their evil plot was to frighten him into compromise and
to sin against God and before man. Why? So they could bring shame
and reproach upon his name and reputation, before those who were
laboring with him – wanting to stop the plans of God.

If we walk in compromise and mixture, it will stop the plans of
God from going forth in our lives every time. If we are not grounded
in the Word of God, with a lifestyle of prayer – we will easily fall
into compromise and mixture. We will easily be deceived by the
false prophets and teachers that are in our midst, who care only
about promoting their own selfish agenda. We may end up building
something, but it will not be His plans for us. It will be wood, hay and
stubble – all dead works that will not have lasting eternal fruit.

1 CORINTHIANS 3:11-13
*For no other foundation can anyone lay than that which
is laid, which is Jesus Christ. Now if anyone builds on*

this foundation with gold, silver, precious stones, wood, hay, straw, each one's work will become clear; for the Day will declare it, because it will be revealed by fire; and the fire will test each one's work, of what sort it is.

We see, though, that Nehemiah did not fall for the false prophet's lies, nor could he be manipulated by them. He did not run! Instead, he confronted the lies head on – calling them for what they were. So too should be our response – fearless and fearsome, when facing the false leadership in these last days. To confront their lies with the sword of truth, and not give into the fear that these spirits want to control us with, because we will not obey their evil counsel.

We see these same spirits operating in the Church today. They influence believers to bring false reports – creating fear, confusion and division, and causing many to walk in compromise and to sin against God. And, at the same time, they bring shame and reproach upon those who are building God's way. Remember, Sanballat and Tobiah hired the false prophet – it was pre-meditated evil. They had to think about what they were doing – it was not an accident.

NEHEMIAH 6:10-12 AMP.

I went into the house of Shemaiah son of Delaiah, the son of Mehetabel, who was shut up. He said, let us meet together in the house of God, within the temple, and let us shut the doors of the temple, for they are coming to kill you—at night they are coming to kill you. But I said, should such a man as I flee? And what man such as I could go into the temple [where only the priests are allowed to go] and yet live? I will not go in. And behold, I saw that God had not sent him, but he made this prophecy against me because Tobiah and Sanballat had hired him.

9. Ultimately, these spirits come to destroy a righteous person's reputation. They do this if all other tactics fail – where they cannot 'physically assassinate' God's plans in our lives. Then in their ruthlessness, they go for the jugular vein. They come to assassinate our character: to destroy our reputation. Not that it should ever be about our reputation being elevated – heaven forbid, for we are to go low and stay hidden in Christ. But God has His chosen and anointed ones to do His will. We see that with Nehemiah. He was God's chosen and anointed one to do the work at hand.

So too, in our day, God has His anointed and chosen vessels to do His work in the nations. If these evil spirits can destroy their reputation, it will be the fastest way to stop God's plans from going forth, for no one will want to labor with them. Gossip, slander and accusation of the brethren are the primary spirits that operate under the spirits of Sanballat and Tobiah [Nehemiah 6:13].

NEHEMIAH 6:13 AMP.
He was hired that I should be made afraid and do as he said and sin, that they might have matter for an evil report with which to taunt and reproach me.

Ministry of Constant Warfare

Soon after my arrival in Ireland, in October 2015, the Lord commissioned me to raise up 32 houses of prayer – one in every county, by raising up intercessors who will build His way. Then in January 2018, we were commissioned by the Lord to do a prayer meeting in every county. It was a long, hard road of ploughing up hard, fallow ground, that was to be completed in twelve months. It was no easy assignment and we faced constant warfare. For two of our meetings, I was to co-labor with another ministry, who was to bring forth a teaching that I had believed would help the laborers unite, arise and build.

Shortly, after this couple arrived, it became apparent that the enemy wanted to destroy the meetings, the ministry and this relationship, by bringing a bad report from others about me. After listening to what this sister shared from others, I felt condemned, as well as unfairly accused, as the source that was accusing me, remained hidden behind her voice. For she was not willing to say who this bad report was coming from. Instead she believed the report, without asking what my experiences may have been with those who were now my accusers. I was just broken inside, knowing we face such warfare, and the enemy hates that we are a prayer ministry.

Accusation of the Brethren

To bring accusations from others is not a good situation to find ourselves in, and, if there is to be an impartial, productive and restorative dialogue to come forth, both sides need to be represented. But even better, we should avoid being a vessel that can be used by Satan in this evil way. For it only creates division, when it is not approached in this manner. It will not bring restoration and has the potential to destroy other people's lives and destinies.

To say the least, it was a difficult situation. The irony of it was that this dear sister had fallen into the very snares of the enemy that she was coming to teach on – to help bring unity to the laborers. She had believed reports that were twisted and distorted, which character-assassinated me. But when in reality, it was nothing less than gossip and slander, hiding behind 'masked identities' that had influenced her.

That night as I sat before the Lord in tears, feeling so blindsided, I prayed for great grace to overcome this attack His way. I knew that walking in complete humility and obedience was going to be vital for me to do so. I could not help but question how this mature believer had listened to this evil blindly. How she could have believed those reports, without talking to me first?

A Flood of Evil

I soon went into battle in prayer. For a flood of evil had come upon the ministry. After some time, I asked, *"Lord, how do You feel about this – what was spoken?"* As I waited, I soon found myself in a dream. In the dream, there were two women in a corridor talking with each other. There was a door in the middle of the corridor that was halfway open, and it led to where I do not know. I could see it was completely dark, and the sister that had now turned against me was in that place – covered in darkness.

That morning I shared the dream. I did not have its understanding, nor did she. But it became known to me in the days to come. The Lord revealed that what took place was not of Him. Because she listened to the evil reports, in that very moment a seed was sown into her mind. If she had rejected that information, it would not have become ill-fruit in her heart towards me. But once that seed went from her mind – a thought, into her heart, she was no longer able to be impartial. It caused her to go into a place of darkness, where she was deceived and believed the evil report.

2 CORINTHIANS 10:4-5
For the weapons of our warfare are not carnal but mighty in God for pulling down strongholds, casting down arguments and every high thing that exalts itself against the knowledge of God, bringing every thought into captivity to the obedience of Christ.

The two women in the corridor who were talking with each other, were wolves in sheep's clothing. This deception came upon this sister because of witchcraft, and from those who were in her sphere of influence. She was not able to discern that their motives towards her ministry and mine were for evil. Because of it, they were able to deflect and reflect the attention away from themselves, by their spells and curses, and they put the blame onto others – me. Their motive was to destroy not only this relationship, but all eternal relationships for the ministry.

Gossip and Slander are Deadly

Gossip and slander are deadly, not only to our relationship with the Lord, but to those in our path. As a believer, we should not even entertain one whisper. And if we do, we need to repent. We have all found ourselves in situations where a conversation turns to gossip or slander. But as soon as those whispering spirits start to share an evil report about another, our job is to stop it in its tracks – to say lovingly, *"Please stop. What you are doing is wrong – it is sin. If you have an issue with someone, please speak to them directly, or say nothing."*

It does not mean that we do not talk about the sin and issues that takes place in our spheres of influence. But we need do it in a godly, righteous way, where we are not listening to or promoting gossip and slander. But rather, we are sincerely seeking truth in a matter by seeking the Lord in prayer asking for His wise counsel. We need to come with a heart posture not to tear down another man or woman's character or reputation. We have to address the sin, the hard things that take place before our eyes, without character assassination.

Most believers are not mature enough to stop their flesh from indulging in gossip and slander. Often, people gossip and slander under the guise of needing prayer. We need to know though, that it does not matter if the report is true or not; as a believer, we have to guard our lips. For when we partake in it, the reality is that we are killing one another spiritually and stopping God's work from going forth. The damage has been done, and it is often impossible to undo.

Gossip and slander often happen because of these workers of darkness, dressed in sheep's clothing, who are in our midst, putting spells and curses on us. They come to pollute, defile, infect and affect us with their evil. Their purpose: not only to character-assassinate a person's reputation, but to cause division, with the goal to destroy the eternal relationships that are meant to rebuild the broken-down walls together, in the nations.

NEHEMIAH 6:13 AMP.
He was hired that I should be made afraid and do as he said and sin, that they might have matter for an evil report with which to taunt and reproach me.

A Wounded Warrior

Today, we too are facing the same wicked spirits that Nehemiah faced. These spirits come to attack, especially those who are building according to God's plans. Those who are building up the wall and standing in the gap before the Lord, in that place of intercession, so that He would not have to destroy the land [Ezekiel 22:30]. Those who are fighting the good fight of faith in word, thought and deed, though not perfect in all their ways, but faithful to the call. They are fighting so that He can redeem and restore nations back to their rightful identity that can only be found in Him.

But too often when in battle, we take it personally – we get offended, or become fearful. We look at the people – the circumstances that are in front of us. We forget that we wrestle not against flesh and blood. And because of it, we disengage from the battle as a wounded warrior.

2 TIMOTHY 2:3
You therefore must endure hardship as a good soldier of Jesus Christ.

Nehemiah recognised that he was not wrestling against flesh and blood. If he had not, he would not have responded the way he did, and that is the difference. Nehemiah responded according to the Spirit of the Living God. He did not react according to his flesh. And because of it, he was able to rebuild the broken-down walls in record time!

The spirits of Sanballat and Tobiah operate wherever there is a real prayer movement of God taking place. One that has one agenda – His agenda, to rebuild the broken-down walls in the nations. These spirits come to stop the intercessors from uniting. If they cannot mock, shame, condemn, seduce or put fear into us, then they go for the jugular vein and attack with character assassination. If we are not mature believers, we will not recognise their tactics. Instead, we become their prey, and God's plans will not go forth in our lives, cities and nations.

How Should We Respond to These Attacks?

First, we have to recognise these spirits by their modes of operation. And that we wrestle not with flesh and blood. That the battle will mostly be won in that place of prayer – where we get understanding and strategies for our next steps. Having a consistent prayer life will help to recognise the attacks for what they are, and the source of evil that feeds them. When we do, we will end up walking after the spirit, and not reacting according to our flesh

Remember Paul and Silas in Acts chapter 16. When they were on their way to a prayer meeting, they were harassed by a witch who had followed them for days. Paul and Silas never made the prayer meeting. They ended up in prison instead, after Paul dismantled that spirit of divination that was operating, trying to hinder the work they were called to do.

ACTS 16:16-18

Now it happened, as we went to prayer, that a certain slave girl possessed with a spirit of divination met us, who brought her masters much profit by fortune-telling. This girl followed Paul and us, and cried out, saying, "These men are the servants of the Most High God, who proclaim to us the way of salvation." And this she did for many days.

Satan despises those who pray. He comes to hinder and stop our prayers any way he can, and primarily through workers of darkness that are in our midst. The enemy thought he could retaliate against Paul for setting that slave girl free from the spirit of divination. Paul paid a price for confronting and casting out the evil that was in his midst. But the Lord used it for good. In their place of captivity, a great shaking took place. It took place because Paul and Silas were not moved by their flesh, after the onslaught of evil against them, but continued to pray and worship. This caused a great shaking and awakening to take place, resulting in the prison guard and his entire household being saved [Acts 16:25-34].

We see that when Sanballat and Tobiah heard that Nehemiah was rebuilding, they mocked and scorned him, believing they could stop him. But Nehemiah's response was, *"The God of heaven will prosper us. Therefore, we His servants will arise and build"* [Nehemiah 2:20]. So too should be our response – not to back down from the battle, but to engage in it. But to engage God's way!

A Call to Engage in the Battle

Nehemiah set up a Watch, day and night, 24-hours, seven days a week, against their evil schemes. He called for all laborers to unite and fight for the brethren, for their families, for their homes – for their nation to be saved. It was a call to war – to engage in the battle. It was all hands-on deck, laboring with one hand, while wielding their sword with the other, until the wall was rebuilt. If they had not united, their enemies would have defeated them and stopped the wall from being rebuilt [Nehemiah 4:9, 14, 17].

NEHEMIAH 4:9 AMP.
*But because of them we made our prayer to our God
and set a watch against them day and night.*

Nehemiah was a true, selfless, fearless, faithful, focused and committed leader, who had one agenda – the Lord's agenda: for his people to be restored to truth. For them to be restored back to righteousness and the Lord's ways of doing things. He refused to walk in compromise, or in the fear of man. And because of it, he had discernment. He did not fall for his enemies' traps. He confronted their lies and slander with truth – every single time, putting to flight their evil counsel. Nehemiah was not silent when faced with the evil that wanted to destroy them [Nehemiah 6:3, 8, 11].

So too, the Lord expects us not to stay silent or walk in fear of man. Often, we walk in fear of man doing what pleases man, and not

God. Our silence, by not engaging in the battle, is not going to set our nations free from the anti-Christ governments that are hell-bent on destroying us with the iron-clad grip of the spirit of Pharaoh.

When we unite in truth, that is what will set us free. Nehemiah was able to unite the laborers in truth, and despite man's and Satan's plans, the wall was built in record time. It caused the fear of the Lord to come upon the nations [1 Thessalonians 2:4, Nehemiah 6:16].

We need to be like Nehemiah, keeping the full armor of God on day and night, that we may stand the evil day. That we would rebuild the broken-down walls, starting first in our marriages, in our relationships – for it has to start there, before we can effectively rebuild the broken-down walls in our cites and nations. AMEN!

CHAPTER 5

JEZEBEL AND ASHTORETH

I know your works, love, service, faith, and your patience; and as for your works, the last are more than the first. Nevertheless, I have a few things against you, because you allow that woman Jezebel, who calls herself a prophetess, to teach and seduce My servants to commit sexual immorality and eat things sacrificed to idols. And I gave her time to repent of her sexual immorality, and she did not repent. Indeed, I will cast her into a sickbed, and those who commit adultery with her into great tribulation, unless they repent of their deeds. I will kill her children with death, and all the churches shall know that I am He who searches the minds and hearts. And I will give to each one of you according to your works [Revelation 2:19-23].

Spiritual Wickedness in Heavenly Places

There are many teachings and others more qualified than I, who can help us understand Jezebel and Ashtoreth, these wicked rulers of darkness who are spiritual wickedness in heavenly places. The spirits of Sanballat and Tobiah work in conjunction with Jezebel, who is their boss. And they target mainly those who are building God's plans, His way. But Jezebel on the other hand, targets everyone – saved and unsaved. She is no respecter of persons! And all of their works, though, are rooted in the occult. So why focus on this, one might ask? Because it is what the true Church has been facing and will face greatly in these last days.

This witchcraft coming from Jezebel and Ashtoreth is the 'root' and 'fuel' of the apostasy that we have been seeing in the Church. It is only going to get much more wicked. It will be the Church's final and greatest battle to overcome. When Elijah slew the 450 false prophets of Baal, he did not slay the 400 false prophets of Jezebel, who dined at her table. That work has been left for this last generation to complete. For those same wicked spirits have infiltrated the Church, and have been operating in the Church ever since.

This battle will be fierce and not for the faint-hearted! It will cause the separating of the wheat from the tares – the true church from the false church, and will eventually usher in the Lord's soon Second Coming and return. If you are not aware of the witchcraft that is found in just about every church meeting or Christian gathering these days, and you do not know how to discern its workings and how to stand against it, you will be deceived. You will miss fulfilling the high call that is on your life. For that is their goal, all the while trying to stop the Lamb from receiving the reward of His suffering in the fullest measure, which is for the nations to be saved.

Witchcraft in the Church

Witchcraft is in just about every church – every meeting that takes place. Wherever Jezebel resides, you can be certain that there are workers of darkness hiding in the shadows, working their magic, trying to destroy the true prophetic voice and the plans of God for our lives. Many who say they are a 'Christian' are really wolves dressed in sheep's clothing. They look, sound and act like Christians. I have had the blessed opportunity to meet several along the way, all by the Lord's divine design, to teach and train me how to fight against this evil in prayer.

In 2009, when I came into the understanding of the prophetic call that is upon every believer's life, I joined a small group of believers that met weekly and moved in the prophetic. The prophetic was all new to me, and the woman who led the group befriended me quickly with a 'word' for me. She was a 'worship leader' with many connections with churches in the Greater Phoenix area. She followed Bethel in Redding, California, which at the time I did not know anything about their teachings and practices.

I partook in these weekly meetings for about a year and a half. At the same time, I was spending a lot more time in the Word, praying and waiting on the Lord pursuing with fervency the high and lofty destiny that the Lord had for me. During this time though, I kept getting checks in my spirit about some of the things that were taking place. But because it was all relatively new to me, I could not pinpoint exactly what was wrong.

This woman and her friend, who were the leaders of this group, would say things like, *"If you see a 'light' go and stand in it."* They were implying that a spiritual transference – an encounter would take place, and you did not want to miss it. They always had a word for someone, and it often felt manipulating to me. They belittled the powers of darkness, as if they were a laughing matter.

They were chasing after 'spiritual experiences' and encouraging others to do so, without the teaching of sanctification and consecration. I was naïve at best, but the Lord had given me discernment, even though at that time I did not know how to use it wisely. I knew things were not right, but I kept going, and would brush aside the times I felt that check.

During this time the Lord gave me a dream, where I saw these two women's faces and a man of God, who I knew to be a true prophet of the Lord. He was pointing his finger and saying to me very sternly that they were witches. When I awoke, I thought it was the enemy trying to get me to think evil. So, although I did not forget that dream, I pushed it to the side, not wanting to falsely accuse them or to think evil about them, feeling horrible for doing so.

They Treated His Glory Cheaply

Several months later, after one more strange time of worship together, I knew I was not to return, for what they were doing was not okay. It did not display the Lord's holiness or any fear of the Lord.

Instead, they treated His glory cheaply. Like a vending machine, where we can put a few coins in and make a selection and get what we want. That was the analogy I had that day, and I was sickened inside that I had been deceived by their strange practices. To make it worse, there were a few dear friends of mine, who went to this group and thought highly of these women. I parted ways, obeying the voice of the Lord, Who was speaking to my spirit, saying that I was not to return. But I had nothing in the natural to back it up – so how could I say anything to anyone?

I tried to distance myself from this woman, which was not easy. She wanted to stay involved in my life, which I resisted as much as I could. When the Lord called me to a church that I was to be in for a season, this woman and her husband showed up – just once. When I was called to start a home fellowship and start teaching the Word of God on a weekly basis to the few lambs that I had led to the Lord, she found out and came to the first meeting, but never came again.

At that point, I was not naïve, but still questioned whether I was wrong for I did not want to think this way, feeling accusatory and judgmental for doing so. But I prayed over that meeting and my apartment in every way that I knew how, with the blood of the Lamb, to destroy all witchcraft assigned to destroy what God wanted to do. I knew that the enemy would love to destroy these meetings. For that is what these workers of darkness do. They will find a way to get close to those who are sold out for Jesus, wanting to destroy them and His plans. Sometimes they only come once to the new beginnings in our lives, as they think they can come and put their magic on the good fruit that is to come forth and cause it to dry up. Soon after this woman attended our first meeting, the Lord reminded me of that dream and spoke clearly that it was true – these two women, who say they are Christians, are really witches!

At this point, He instructed me to cut all contact. This meant I was to delete all old emails and any phone numbers from my phone and computer files. As soon as I did, all my contacts on my phone and computer disappeared! Some bewitching powers were not happy that I finally got it and had cut their wicked ties trying to gain access to my life!

Remember, one was a 'worship leader' who moved in and out of many different churches and activities taking place in the community. Can you imagine the damage that has been done to those churches because of this? How many eternal relationships and marriages have been destroyed because this woman had been allowed to profane that holy position in the sanctuary?

At that time, this was all new training for me. Ever since, the Lord speaks very clearly to me, mostly through dreams – sometimes through visions and encounters, warning me of the dangers of others. Often, that is all that will be given for me to discern when I feel a check, but not much in the natural to back it up. He is faithful to protect and enlighten the eyes of our hearts' understanding when we seek Him in prayer, fasting, and from a consecrated lifestyle.

Deceived by Her Magic

There was another time, about six months after I arrived in Ireland, that I met a woman, who I thought was like-minded and spirited. She had a heart for prayer. She sought out those who were praying in the land, and it is why our paths crossed more often. She moved in the prophetic and was very involved in the activities taking place in different groups. I had invited her to some of our meetings, and to the Feast of the Lord gatherings that I had hosted. Initially, I was deceived by her magic – I was blinded to it. Although I was initially deceived, these times were always a revelation to me. I would see that which most people did not see in the spirit, causing me to question the Lord often, asking, *"Who is this woman Lord – is she friend or foe? I do not want to be deceived as I was with those other two women."*

This woman was very controlling. After getting an email from her, wanting to control one of our prayer meetings and how we were to pray, I fervently pursued the Lord again, asking, *"Lord, who is she – friend or foe? I have to know!?"* I soon fell asleep and dreamed that I was standing on a beach, about to wade in the water, when I saw a shark swimming in very shallow water where I was about to go. When I awoke, the Holy Spirit spoke that the shark represented this woman.

So, if you know there is a shark swimming in shallow water, the last thing you would do is to get in the water with it! I was grateful for this warning. My spiritual radar was tuned into this woman even more, but I had nothing in the natural to back up the discernment I had been given.

During this time, a vital eternal relationship fell apart, because of a Jezebel spirit operating within her – wanting to manipulate and control the will of others. The other party that was involved had been spell-bound and blinded by her actions. Therefore, they were unable to see the damage she was causing to our relationship, despite my attempt to speak with them. About a year later, and solely because of prayer to contend for this relationship to be restored, the Lord brought restoration. But it came after this woman was no longer a part of their fellowship.

After several more months, though, another serious situation took place within the ministry with this woman. I went to the Lord in prayer, pleading, *"Lord, I have to know who this woman is clearly – clearer than a shark in shallow water."* I was more tired than usual that day, and went to rest for an hour, when the Lord showed me clearly. In a dream, I saw this woman placing spells and curses on me. I then awoke. I was relieved to finally know who she was, yet sickened again at how evil and relentless the enemy is in his pursuit to destroy us.

Her Purpose was to Destroy

This woman was a wolf dressed in sheep's clothing. Her purpose was to destroy me and the ministry – the houses of prayer that we are called to raise up. She was known in the Christian circles that she moved in and out of, where everyone thought she was a Christian. After the first dream, where I saw a shark in shallow water, I would observe her doings from afar, while avoiding her entrapments. I would break off her spells and curses off everyone, saying nothing to anyone, but praying about it all.

She moved around from one group after another, leaving destruction behind. That was the consistent pattern that I saw.

Whenever I heard she was a part of so and so's group, I would pray for those in charge not to be deceived. For the Lord to protect the eternal relationships. The Lord eventually moved her away, and I cannot say it was a moment too soon!

I have great pity and compassion for those who have chosen to serve Satan's agenda. I pray often for their salvation and deliverance, as we should. I take no joy in seeing a single soul lost or destroyed. But the sad truth is that most of these workers of darkness have no intention of repenting or turning from their wicked ways. They hate God and us with a vengeance and will go to any lengths to hurt us – spiritually, physically, emotionally and financially.

Beloved, we are in a real battle – a real war. And when in war, there are casualties. These are just the hard facts. Often, when I am pressed up against a wall with these Satanists that come to destroy the plans of God, I say, *"Lord, we are in war. If they continue to refuse to repent and turn from their wicked ways, then either they go – or I go, but I can tell You Lord, I have no intention of going, so they must go. I am not willing to die before it is my time!"* The truth is they come to kill and destroy any way they can, and most in the Church let them, willingly, for they have been deceived by them. These are not His plans for us!

Enforcing the Victory of the Cross

There are more experiences to share, and primarily why this book was to be written. Why share them? Because most in the Church do not believe that Christians can be affected by these occultic powers. Or, if they do believe, then they do not think we need to do anything about it – that Jesus did it all for us on the Cross.

The work Jesus did on the Cross is a finished work – there is nothing we can add to it. But He gave us the Holy Spirit to convict us of our sin, to teach us righteousness, and to forewarn of His coming judgments, with the goal to lead us into all truth. The Lord expects every believer to enforce the victory of the Cross.

2 Timothy 2:4-5
No one engaged in warfare entangles himself with the affairs of this life, *that he may please him who enlisted him as a soldier. And also if anyone competes in athletics,* ***he is not crowned unless he competes according to the rules.***

We enforce the victory by engaging in the battle. By taking back the land that has been defiled with compromise, mixture and every ungodly perversion, and we occupy it until His soon Second Coming, starting in our own lives first. For if we do not come out of Babylon completely, we leave our spiritual doors wide open to be deceived. We will not be able to stand against these evil days and enforce the victory of the Cross.

Most believers are bewitched and beguiled, seeing family relationships, church and ministry relationships and God's plans for their lives fall apart. They do not realise that there are real workers of darkness, known as Satanists operating in their midst. Their sole purpose is to destroy the true prophetic voice, and God's plans any way they can. Jezebel will be the initiator of their works, all steeped in witchcraft with the many different masks that she hides behind.

She Thinks She is a Queen Who Sits Upon a Throne

Many years ago, while preparing a teaching for a meeting, the word of the Lord came to me, saying, *"She thinks she is a queen who sits upon a throne."* While pondering who the Lord was referring to – my spirit was quickened, and it became clear it was Jezebel. And it was clear that she needed to be 'dethroned' from the seat of power that she uses to bewitch and beguile the Church, at large.

REVELATION 18:7 AMP.
To the degree that she glorified herself and reveled in her wantonness [living deliciously and luxuriously], to that measure impose on her torment and anguish and

*tears and mourning. **Since in her heart she boasts, I
am not a widow; as a queen [on a throne] I sit,** and I
shall never see suffering or experience sorrow.*

So let us take a closer look at Jezebel and understand a little more about who she is, why her power is so great over so many, and who her primary target is in these last days. But before we do, l want to take a look at Sanballat and Tobiah's family history. So we can see how deep this web is that has been woven by these two spirits that are rooted in witchcraft.

The first mention of Sanballat was in Nehemiah 2:10. He was known as 'the Horonite.' Horonite is a reference to the Moabite city of Horonaim where Sanballat was from [Isaiah 15:5, Jeremiah 48:5, 34]. So, Sanballat was a Moabite and Tobiah was an Ammonite.

We see that the Moabites and Ammonites were connected to Israel through unlawful marriages [Nehemiah 6:18, 13:28]. The Moabites and Ammonites were both distant relatives of the Jews, originating from incestuous relationships between Lot and his daughters. Lot's oldest daughter named her son Moab, who is the father of the Moabites to this day. And Lot's younger daughter named her son Ben-Ammi, who is the father of the Ammonites to this day [Genesis 19:36-38].

We also see that Balak, the king of the Moabites, was the one who hired Balaam to curse God's people – the Jews. Because of it, there became a law that no Ammonite or Moabite was to be allowed into the assembly of the Lord [Nehemiah 13:1-2, Deuteronomy 23:3-4]. This law was to protect Israel from being defiled by the Moabite's lewd practices and pagan worship, which were steeped in sexual immorality and witchcraft. It was to prevent any sorcerers, soothsayers and diviners from having access to the Sanctuary. Peter spoke about these practices.

2 Peter 2:15-16 AMP.

*Forsaking the straight road they have gone astray;
they have followed the way of Balaam [the son] of
Beor, who loved the reward of wickedness. But he was*

rebuked for his own transgression when a dumb beast of burden spoke with human voice and checked the prophet's madness.

Moabites and Ammonites Rooted in Witchcraft

So, who were the Moabites and Ammonites? They were Shemites, who worshipped the same Canaanite gods that Nimrod worshipped. Therefore, they partook in the same wicked practices I shared earlier in chapter 1. They primarily worshipped Molech, Baal and Ashtoreth, who are known by other names. But these are the names that most would know them by.

Molech was an evil deity who they offered child sacrifices to, as fire offerings [Leviticus 18:21, 20:2-4]. Ashtoreth is a female demon connected with the moon, fertility, lewd sexual immorality and war. She is also known as the Queen of Heaven. Those who worship and pray to 'Mary' in the Roman Catholic Church are really worshipping this evil demonic goddess. The Babylonians and Assyrians knew her as Ishtar. Baal was a sun and fertility god, who would be Ashtoreth's male counterpart.

So, the Moabites and Ammonites pagan worship was rooted and saturated in witchcraft, sorcery, divination and soothsaying, all greatly angering the Lord. We see this with King Ahab who was more evil than any king in Israel, prior to him.

1 KINGS 16:33 AMP.
And Ahab made an Asherah [idolatrous symbol of the goddess Asherah]. Ahab did more to provoke the Lord, the God of Israel, to anger than all the kings of Israel before him.

Ahab married Jezebel, who was a Phoenician princess, a Canaanite. She was the daughter of King Ethbaal of Sidonia, which is another name for Phoenicia. She was of royal birth, but her name in

Hebrew can actually mean 'not exalted.'[16] The Sidonians worshipped Baal and Ashtoreth.

The name 'Ethbaal' means 'with him is Baal.' King Ethbaal, Jezebel's father, was also the high priest of Ashtoreth, who was also goddess and consort of Ba'al, in Tyre. The spirit of Ashtoreth came upon Jezebel and possessed her from the day she was born, as her father would have dedicated her at birth to Ashtoreth. It is why she was so wicked and full of sorcery.[17]

Jezebel Served Ashtoreth Faithfully

Like her father, she was a priestess of Ashtoreth whom she served faithfully. The offering of blood sacrifices was a delight and it came as second nature. Every morning, while she was growing up under her father's care, she would go to the temple of Baal and Ashtoreth within the palace grounds. With the priests and prophets of Baal and Ashtoreth, she would burn incense to these idols. She was carefully schooled in the ways of idol worship and witchcraft by them.[18]

Ahab provoked the Lord to anger more than any other king, because he built altars to Baal and Ashtoreth, causing God's people to follow false gods and to become defiled with their pagan, occultic worship. This was not a good mixed marriage – it was lethal! Jezebel was a blood thirsty, false prophetess, who worshipped Ashtoreth and Baal. She killed the true prophets of the Lord, while her 850 false prophets who ate at her table of idolatry, arose in their place [1 Kings 16:30-33, 18:4, 19, Revelation 2:20].

Her goal today is the same as it was in the days of Elijah: to kill the true prophets of the Lord. She aims to kill and destroy the true prophetic voice any way she can. That includes prophetic churches, prophetic ministries and prophetic intercessors. If you are in one of these groups, you can be certain Jezebel has been trying to silence your voice, labeling you as the false voice. She has tried to seduce and deceive you, injure you, financially destroy you, manipulate and control you with her bewitchment and beguilement, and everyone else who is to be a part of your God-given sphere of influence. All these schemes are trying to ruin you spiritually, physically, emotionally, financially – and ultimately your reputation, trying to stop you and others from laboring together.

Most do not realize that Jezebel and Ashtoreth work together, with Ashtoreth hiding behind Jezebel's many masks. They are a lethal spiritual combination and what the true Church – the End-times Army of the Lord, is going to contend with in these last days; both Jezebel and Ashtoreth at the same time – a double dose, so to speak!

Ashtoreth Comes to Steal the Anointing

Ashtoreth, while often hiding behind Jezebel, comes to steal the anointing that is upon one's life. A true prophet of the Lord shared an encounter he had, where the Lord showed him what happened to Saul and why he fell.[19] He was shown how his armor was taken by Ashtoreth and put in her temple of demons. How that is what causes a man or woman of God to fall.

Days before I had heard about this encounter, I had a dream. In the dream, I was in a meeting with other believers. There were many people, but I could only see myself and another woman. I was on my knees, in the front, like I had been praying. This other woman was standing over me, and placed her hands on my head, and while looking at the people, loudly said, *"False anointing, false anointing, false anointing."* I quickly got to my feet, pulling myself away from her and was very upset. By her doing that, I knew two things were taking place. First, it told those who had gathered that I was operating under a false anointing. Therefore, discrediting me and ruining my reputation. Second, as she spoke those false words over me, I knew her intent was to destroy the anointing that was on my life. End of dream.

REVELATION 3:11 AMP.
*I am coming quickly; hold fast what you have, so that
no one may rob you and deprive you of your crown.*

When I awoke, I knew this was a warning to me, and that woman was a witch, trying to curse me with the mantra that she repeated three times. It is exactly what they do. They 'conceal and mask their identity' – their works of darkness, by reflecting and deflecting the attention off of themselves, and put it onto others. This witch's goal was to destroy the true anointing, by the false anointing of witchcraft, which is her source of power. It was a two-fold action. First, outward – for others to see. And second, inward – trying to destroy the gifts and anointing.

If I had not been aware of their tactics, and pray regularly – praying almost daily to break their spells and curses that are crafted to conceal and mask their identity, while reflecting and deflecting the attention from themselves and onto others, I would not have understood the meaning of this dream, nor its warning. I understood that there was another occultic assignment wanting to destroy my reputation, and the anointing on my life. I was then able to pray effectively against this evil, destroying its works.

As Christians, we should not only ask the Lord to protect us from the evil one, but to ask Him to reveal the snakes and vipers that are in our path. And to ask Him to give us heaven's counsel that we would respond according to the Spirit, and not react according to our flesh. So that we would cut the serpent's head off every time – instantaneously, and not waver. If we are not asking, He will not randomly give these kinds of dreams or visions to us, without a relationship that pursues His counsel for every step we take.

Why? Because if He does, we would think it was just an odd dream, and nothing more. He gives dreams, visions and revelation to us, so that we will pray about what we are shown. So, if we are not asking for Him to reveal the evil schemes of the wicked one in our lives, we would not know that He is trying to forewarn us, and that He wants us to pray against this evil. We would end up doing nothing more with it. So the Lord will not pour out revelation in our lives for it to be purposeless.

The Lord does not want anyone to be bewitched and beguiled, or to be caught off guard. He wants us to know their evil schemes.

Not to be fearful of them, but so we will know how to battle against them in prayer, causing our steps to align with His perfect will for our lives. For when He does reveal their wicked schemes, we should seek His counsel in how to pray and how to respond to what is shown. Seekers will be finders and finders will be seekers. When we do, we will receive strategy from heaven that knows no defeat! But if we are not willing to engage in the battle, we limit His ability to equip us, that will enable us to stand against their evil works.

Witches in a Prayer Meeting

Years ago, while leading corporate prayer for a church in Phoenix, there were two witches that attended regularly. Initially, I did not know they were witches, but had discerned something was not right with them. As time went on and several months later, I eventually confronted them with their sorcery letting them know they needed to burn all their occultic books, abandon their ways and turn in repentance to the Lord Jesus Christ. They were literally speechless that someone had called them out for what they were. At the time, I did not know what more to do with them – other than pray against their counsel.

Prior to our talk, though, during one of the meetings, I was on my knees praying. At one point, I felt led to open my eyes. When I did, one of these witches was standing about two feet from me, with her hand stretched out to lay it on the top of my head. I did not stop praying, instead I fell backwards to avoid her touching my head. While looking at her, shaking my head to not touch me.

These workers of darkness will try to touch our head, if possible. Why? Because that part of our body represents, our mind, our will, our emotions – our intellect. They place their hands on our heads to do their magic, wanting to control our will with their will. They use such things as death oil or death water, that represents endings – the end of our thought life, with the goal to destroy the anointing. Be so careful who you allow to lay hands on your head!

I have had other dreams where I have seen witches placing their magic on godly, prophetic pastors and true prophets of the Lord. Why am I shown these things? So that I will pray for this witchcraft to be broken off their lives.

Beloved, we have not yet experienced the level of evil that is coming to the Church, with the manifestation of the combination of Jezebel and Ashtoreth. Are we prepared? Who in the Church, at large, is preparing for it? Who will even talk about such things? To be informed is one way to be armed, and that will help us to be prepared!

Elijah Boldly Confronted Sin

In 1 Kings chapter 18, we see Elijah boldly confronted the sins of his people, out of his zealous love for the Lord – for truth and righteousness! Calling them to make a decision that day – how long will they waver between two opinions? Saying, if the Lord is God, follow Him. But if Baal than follow him. Elijah was calling them out of mixture – out of the lewd pagan worship that they had embraced.

> **1 KINGS 18:21**
> *And Elijah came to all the people, and said, "How long will you falter between two opinions? If the Lord is God, follow Him; but if Baal, follow him." But the people answered him not a word.*

At the same time, he fearlessly confronted the 450 prophets of Baal and the 400 prophets of Ashtoreth, who all dined at Jezebel's table. For years, every time I read these scriptures, I always thought Elijah had killed all 850 false prophets in that great showdown. But if we look closer, we see that he only killed the 450 prophets of Baal [1 Kings 18:40].

We see later the same 400 prophets of Ashtoreth actively involved with Ahab and Jehoshaphat, the king of Judah, when Ahab wants him to go to war with him against the king of Syria over Ramoth-gilead. Jehoshaphat, a wise man, wants Ahab to first inquire a word from the Lord, before committing to go into battle with him. So, what does Ahab do? Instead of seeking the Lord, he calls the 400 false prophets together to seek a word from them [1 Kings 22:5-6].

Ahab was Under the Control of Jezebel

Why did Ahab seek the false prophets and not the Lord? It is a direct result of his mixed marriage to Jezebel and how deadly her influence was over him. Ahab knew truth. He knew who the true Living God was but was living in mixture. He was under the control of Jezebel – under her spells, her seduction, her influences, that were able to bewitch and beguile him. To the point where he really believed he could walk in compromise and it would end well for him [1Kings 21:25].

But we see that was not the case for either Ahab or Jezebel, after they stole what did not belong to them – Naboth's vineyard. Ahab wanted it, but Naboth was not willing to give it up. Therefore, Jezebel takes over, and by lying and falsely accusing Naboth, she has him stoned to death. All to get what she wants – Naboth's vineyard for her husband. Elijah shows up on the scene and prophesies both their deaths [1 Kings 21].

But we cannot blame Jezebel for everything. She can only influence to the degree we allow. Ahab was by no means an innocent bystander. Jezebel was able to influence and control him, because of the idols of his heart that he loved more than the Lord God Almighty. She was able to prey on that sin and use it for her wicked gain and to his destruction [1 Kings 21:25].

Jezebel Sits Enthroned Because of Idols in our Hearts

Likewise, it is same for many in the Church today. Because of the idols in our hearts, Jezebel sits enthroned over many believers' lives, and rules in most churches. It is why her power of influence is so great. Most believers today, at best, are lukewarm – carnal Christians, who walk after their flesh, and not after the Spirit; who walk in mixture and compromise by embracing and promoting doctrines of demons. They walk in the false grace teachings that speak of blessing and prosperity that are void of the true Gospel – a call to live the crucified life. These teachings are void of a call to repentance and the forewarnings of judgments to come. They are void of teachings on suffering, and how our sufferings were always meant to transform us into His image and likeness, until Christ is completely formed within our souls [Galatians 4:19].

When our hearts are full of sin – of idolatry – the lusts of the eyes, the lusts of the flesh and pride of life, we are polluting and defiling the Sanctuary of the Lord, with modern-day temple prostitution and strange fire offerings. When we refuse to confront sin boldly, it not only hurts us, but all those in our sphere of influence. It does not mean we become self-righteous in our pursuit of truth and holiness. It means we die daily, with our goal to be conformed to the fruit of the spirit – love, joy, peace, patience, kindness, goodness, faithfulness, humility and self-control [1 Corinthians 15:31, 2 Timothy 4:2, Galatians 5:22-23].

2 Corinthians 6:16-7, 7:1
And what agreement has the temple of God with idols? *For you are the temple of the living God. As God has said: "I will dwell in them and walk among them. I will be their God, and they shall be My people." Therefore "Come out from among them and be separate, says the Lord. Do not touch what is unclean, and I will receive you." Therefore, having these promises, beloved, let us cleanse ourselves from all filthiness of the flesh and spirit, perfecting holiness in the fear of God.*

How Long Will We Waver Between Two Opinions?

Many today have the mindset that we can have both this world and the Kingdom of God. But it is one or the other. We are no different today, than those in the days of Elijah. We all must decide this day, whom will we serve. Are we willing to forsake all other lovers? How long will we waver between two opinions? It is the main reason why the Church, at large, is spell-bound. We have not been willing to let go of the idols of our heart, but instead we enjoy dining at Jezebel's table of idolatry. If we choose mixture, there is a danger that we too can end up like Ahab.

It is also a reason why the false prophets are on the rise, and why there are so many false words in the Church today. They prophesy to the idols of people's hearts, leading them further astray. It is why we need to be grounded in the Word, and living a holy, consecrated lifestyle unto the Lord – in our words, thoughts and deeds. It is why we need to be purified by the Word of God and submissive to His authority. Otherwise, He will hand us over to the idols of our hearts.

We see this with Ahab when he called the 400 prophets of Ashtoreth to give him a word. They gave him a false word. Jehoshaphat would have known that they were false prophets. It is why he asked if there was anyone else that they could ask! Ahab told him there is one man, Macaiah. But he said, *"I hate him!"* That hate came from the spirits of Jezebel and Ashtoreth that were working in his heart. It was the same hate that killed the true prophets. He hated him, because he did not prophesy what Ahab's itching ears wanted to hear. We see something odd though. Macaiah, initially, prophesies the same counsel as the 400 false prophets [1 Kings 22:5-23]. But Ahab knew he was not speaking truth.

Macaiah Prophesied to the Idols in Ahab's Heart

So, why would Macaiah, who was a true prophet of the Lord, do this? On the surface it appears he was lying to Ahab. But if we look at Ezekiel 14:3-4, we will see that Macaiah was not lying. Instead he was prophesying to the idols of Ahab's heart. Why? Because Ahab wanted to stay in mixture. He did not love truth more than the air he breathed.

EZEKIEL 14:3-4

"Son of man, these men have set up their idols in their hearts, and put before them that which causes them to stumble into iniquity. Should I let Myself be inquired of at all by them? **"Therefore speak to them, and say to them, 'Thus says the Lord God: "Everyone of the house of Israel who sets up his idols in his heart,** *and puts before him what causes him to stumble into iniquity,* **and then comes to the prophet, I the Lord will answer him who comes, according to the multitude of his idols.**

It is a serious warning for all who move in the prophetic to pay heed. That if we are chasing after an experience and not pursuing a relationship first and foremost with the Lord Jesus, by wanting to sit in the Refiner's fire, being purified until our character matches His, we can end up in the occult. Not that we will become witches or warlocks in that sense, but it is that same spirit that will influence our will, causing us to become easy prey to these workers of darkness that are in our midst. All because we have opened our spirit up to these deceiving spirits.

If we chase after an experience and not a relationship, we will have false dreams, visions and words. Others will prophesy over us falsely, not because they are necessarily false prophets, but because they will prophesy to the idols of our heart – what our flesh really wants. We will receive false prayer strategies when in battle, that can lead to our pre-mature demise.

I have heard of meetings where it is advertised that a personal word of prophecy will be given. Encouraging people to sign up early as the 'prophecy slots' fill up quickly. These types of meetings draw a good crowd. The truth is though, that they are nothing less than fortune telling with a spirit of Baalam operating. Merchandising the gifts and the anointing. Prophecy without sanctification and consecration will lead oneself, and others, away from truth, humility, purity, holiness and the fear of the Lord and into the occult directly, or indirectly.

Witchcraft in Governments

This is what we will be contending with in these last days – this lethal spiritual combination of Jezebel and Ashtoreth. We have not yet seen the depths of their evil. Not only in the Church, but in our governments. It is why governments in the nations are saturated in the occult and witchcraft – spiritual wickedness in high places. It has come into our governments, because the Church has flung the doors wide open to it first. It is a spiritual law. Whatever takes place in a government is because it was allowed into the Church first.

> **ISAIAH 1:7 AMP.**
> *[Because of your detestable disobedience] your country lies desolate, your cities are burned with fire; your land — strangers devour it in your very presence, and it is desolate, as overthrown by aliens.*

> **REVELATION 18:23 AMP.**
> *And never again shall the light of a lamp shine in you, and the voice of bridegroom and bride shall never be heard in you again; for your businessmen were the great and prominent men of the earth, and by your magic spells and poisonous charm all nations were led astray (seduced and deluded).*

In May 2016, our nation elected a publicly confessed gay witch. She wrote a book, *The Hope for Wholeness: A Spirituality for Feminists*, where she shares about her spiritual beliefs.[20] She was appointed as Minister of Children and Youth Affairs. As a nation, we had a witch who was responsible for making decisions for our children's welfare. But with fasting and prayer from His praying Remnant this woman was dethroned in the February 2020 elections.

Beloved, these are dark, troubling days of wickedness escalating before our eyes, every day! Again, we love the people with the love of Christ. But we hate the sin and call it for what it is according to the Word of God. As His Ekklesia, the Lord expects us to stand against it and not stay silent. To fight the good fight of faith for these lost souls to be saved, through intercessory prayer, fasting and standing in the gap with identification repentance.

These abominations – types of sin, are in our government because they were allowed into our churches first. We did not confront the sin boldly and boot it out. At large, we did not bring forth the true Gospel of Jesus Christ, in truth and in love to these lost souls, giving them the blessed opportunity to be free from the bondage. Instead we welcome the sinner into our midst, encouraging them to stay in their sinful lifestyle that will only bring them a spiritual death.

Where is the Bride's Voice?

So, where is the Bride's voice – the true Church's voice in this hour? It is so hard to hear it. Many know the truth but remain silent and look the other way. Some, perhaps, think it is not their battle to engage in. Or, if it does not affect them directly, it does not burden their hearts.

I think even worse though, that there are many that believe these abominations are okay – many wavering between two opinions. That is called compromising the Word of God. Many do so, because of fear of man. We see this gaining momentum in the nations, with churches supporting the LGBTQ+ agenda, promoting men and women who are gay into leadership positions, and then come against those who stand against this evil agenda.

LEVITICUS 18:22
You shall not lie with a male as with a woman. It is an abomination.

ROMANS 1:26-27
For this reason God gave them up to vile passions. For

even their women exchanged the natural use for what is against nature. Likewise also the men, leaving the natural use of the woman, burned in their lust for one another, men with men committing what is shameful, and receiving in themselves the penalty of their error which was due.

1 CORINTHIANS 6:9-10

Do you not know that the unrighteous will not inherit the kingdom of God? Do not be deceived. Neither fornicators, nor idolaters, nor adulterers, nor homosexuals, nor sodomites, nor thieves, nor covetous, nor drunkards, nor revilers, nor extortioners will inherit the kingdom of God.

In May 2018, there was a video of an Irish priest having sex with another man on the altar in a church in Kildorrery, Ireland. The irony of this news is that it was a homosexual bishop who reported the incident. He was concerned about the site being 'desecrated' by this sexual act, not concerned about the men's sexual orientation.[21] Sometimes truth is stranger than fiction!

Homosexuality is an abomination to the Lord. It is nothing less than modern day temple prostitution, and it is very active in the Church today. Why is it such an offense to the Holy One? Because the seed of man – his sperm, was to be used to create life when it entered into a woman's egg. That seed was created in the image of His holy Seed. So, when in a gay relationship, that Seed is being spilt and used to produce evil. It is not being used for the Creator's eternal purpose, but to satisfy the lust of man's flesh.

That seed in a gay relationship can never bring forth life – lasting good fruit. It is not only spiritually impossible, but physically impossible, for God did not create men to give birth to children. That Divine order and nature was set apart as holy unto the Lord. It is one of the most amazing mysteries and miracles of all time – how a child is formed in the womb, in His image and likeness! So, Satan always comes to destroy that which the Lord said is to be holy and pure.

Why Are We So Complacent?

So, why are we so complacent? Again, I define complacent as: a feeling of self-satisfaction, unaware of the dangers and deficiencies in us and all around us – having a feeling of false security. I believe it is vastly due to witchcraft that has spellbound the Church, at large, causing deception to come upon many. Causing them to stay in compromise – in sinful lifestyles, truly believing the lies that have been crafted to destroy them. It is why so many walk between two opinions causing them to be lukewarm. There are real powers of darkness operating in the Church, that have one three-fold agenda – to steal, kill and destroy us [John 10:10].

The Opposition Feels Too Great

At the same time, there are so many precious sons and daughters who are powerful and anointed prayer warriors, fighting the good fight of faith, who are engaged in the battle. Yet, often they feel so defeated and discouraged by what is taking place in their lives. Sometimes, they want to give up, for the opposition feels too great at times. Often though, this is because they have become the main target of witchcraft, whether in the Church or outside the Church. That witchcraft has been spoken over their lives, trying to get them to be like Elijah, and not come out of their caves.

Ignorance at times can be bliss. But wisdom and understanding of what we are facing is much better! There is hope and encouragement when we know the source of our afflictions. It may not mean our struggles become easier, for they often will not. But at least we know why the battle is so great – the source of it. We can then seek the Lord for His counsel – prayer strategies, and know how to effectively come against it.

We Are in a Real War!

We are in a real war! And when in war, we need to know the enemy's tactics so we can counterattack and gain the victory. Jezebel's main tactic is to paralyse us with fear, so that she can manipulate, intimidate and dominate our wills, that we would run from the call upon our lives. That was one mistake Elijah made – he ran from Jezebel instead of killing her.

Our war strategies come when we hunker down in our prayer bunkers seeking the Lord for those plans. Prayer is how people, cities and nations get saved. It is what causes the Holy Spirit to come, who causes change to come. It is what births revival and causes a spirit of reformation to come, bringing change to cities and nations on a governmental level.

But not all prayer is the same. There are petitions that are a type of prayer. There are prayers of thanksgiving. Then you have intercessory prayer, where the strategy and outcome are often long-term, with many shorter-term breakthroughs along the way, that bring us steps closer to the final victory – or outcome. There are times, though, where we have shorter intercessory prayer assignments. So intercessory prayer is not one or the other but can be both.

As an intercessor, we aim to know the will of God for a situation. For when we do, we will keep praying until and until the breakthrough comes, or we die – whichever comes first! That is the true heart of an intercessor. They know the will of God and refuse to settle for less. They are often what I describe like a pit bull with a bone in its mouth – refusing to let go of it! And who would be able to snatch that bone out of its mouth, or who in their right mind would even try?

Jezebel Comes to Invoke Fear and Intimidation

In the natural, I don't think anyone would. But in the spirit realm, Jezebel will try any way she can to stop the intercessor's prayers. Because she knows, along with all the hordes of hell, Satan fears a surrendered, consecrated, humble praying vessel. Why? Because the

Lord will use that vessel's intercession to bring forth His plans in the nations. It is one reason why her attacks are so vicious. She comes to invoke fear and intimidation to silence our voice – our prayer life, by paralysing, strangulating, suffocating and immobilising us. Why? Because it is the intercessors – the Remnant, who will sacrificially bow their knees and hearts in prayer, causing the nations to be saved. They pray not for the fame of their name – for most are nameless and faceless, but for the fame of His name to be glorified in the nations, as He alone deserves!

I know of a precious woman, who was new to intercessory prayer on the level that we pray as a ministry. When she would attend our meetings, she would become paralysed and gripped with fear. She would barely be able to speak, because of a tightening that would manifest around her throat. It terrified her as she did not understand what was happening to her.

She would describe it like a noose around her neck. I knew she was called and chosen to be a part of the Lord's End-times Army, and this manifestation was the attack of Jezebel trying to silence her voice. Trying to get her to run from the call that was on her life, and from this ministry that was helping her come into a deeper understanding of the hour that we are in. She was fearless in so many ways, and went on to overcome much, when most would run!

When Jezebel terrified Elijah by threatening to kill him – he ran for his life, and from his call. He sought shelter in a dark cave thinking he would just die. That was the affect Jezebel had over him. Then the Lord asked Elijah twice, *"What are you doing here?"* By asking Him twice, the Lord was emphasising and implying that he was not where he was supposed to be. This is one of Jezebel's tactics, to get us where we are not supposed to be – out the will of God. She wants to drive us into a dark cave, trying to steal our hope and the plans God has for our lives.

Jezebel Power is Like Venom

Jezebel's power is like venom from a snake bite. When that strike enters our heart spiritually, it causes us to become paralysed. The

Lord allowed me to feel this in a very real way. That venom is so oppressive. It makes you want to die – to give up. It makes you feel worthless, causing you to question, what am I doing here? It makes you think that you are a big failure. It makes you want to shut down, shut up and never speak again – in a really evil way. It makes you feel condemned and shamed. These are just some of her wicked tactics.

The Lord had given me a dream, to help me better understand her snake venom. In the dream, I was standing against a wall with my arms at my side but away from my body, like when security does a body search on you at the airport. There were two snake mouths, one over each of my wrists. They had their mouths wide open, displaying their venomous fangs. The width of their mouths covered my wrist, like if someone was going to put handcuffs on you. They did not bite me but it was understood that if I tried to move, they would.

This is the paralysing affect Jezebel can have in wanting to control our lives. If we are not aware of her evil schemes, she bites often and her snake venom is very debilitating. And ultimately, what fuels Jezebel's bite – or power, is witchcraft. Often coming from those disguised in sheep's clothing who move freely in our midst.

So, like the spirits of Sanballat and Tobiah, if Jezebel cannot destroy us physically or emotionally, she goes for the jugular vein. She will use character assassination – gossip and slander, to destroy our name, our families, our churches or ministries. All trying to stop God's plans from going forth in our lives, in our families, cities and nations.

The Spirit and Power of Elijah

But there is hope! The Lord has an awesome and fearsome plan for those engaging in the battle. The spirit and the power of Elijah is being released upon the earth in these last days. Released upon those who are known as the Bride of Christ, the Overcomers – the Sons of God. They will be filled with the Seven Spirits of the Lord, enabling them to engage in the battle, confronting sin boldly [Isaiah 11:2].

ISAIAH 11:2

The Spirit of the Lord shall rest upon Him, the Spirit of wisdom and understanding, the Spirit of counsel and might, the Spirit of knowledge and of the fear of the Lord.

HEBREWS 6:5

And have tasted the good word of God and the powers of the age to come.

They will finish what Elijah failed to do. They will slay Jezebel and destroy her wicked works, that are fueled by Ashtoreth's wicked powers, who are trying to destroy the true prophets of the Lord, and trying to stop the true prophetic voice from going forth from the throne of God. The Bride of Christ will do this by being filled with the powers of the age to come that Paul spoke about in Hebrews. For an in-depth understanding of Jezebel, Ashtoreth, and the spirit and power of Elijah, I highly recommend Brother Sadhu Sundar Selvaraj's book *Elijah is Coming*.[22] It is a must read for anyone who wants to be prepared for these last days! AMEN!

CHAPTER 6

OPENING PORTALS OF PRAYER

Be sober, be vigilant; because your adversary the devil walks about like a roaring lion, seeking whom he may devour. Resist him, steadfast in the faith, knowing that the same sufferings are experienced by your brotherhood in the world [1 Peter 5:8-9].

I want to share a powerful testimony that was a part of Dr. John Mulinde's, *Gems Out of Africa Prayer Teaching Series: Opening the Portals of Prayer – Combat in the Heavenlies.*[23] He shares a testimony from a former Satanist, whose parents at birth had dedicated him to Lucifer, and how he later became a Christian. May these powerful words enlighten the eyes of our hearts' understanding that we would see the spiritual battle that rages against our prayers. May they cause us to engage in the battle even more and not retreat!

Opening the Portals of Prayer – Combat in the Heavenlies
By Dr. John Mulinde

Finally my brethren, be strong in the Lord and in the power of His might. Put on the whole armor of God, that you may be able to stand against the wiles of the devil. Because we wrestle not against flesh and blood but against principalities and powers, and against the rulers of the darkness of this world and against spiritual wickedness in high places. Therefore, take unto you the whole armor of God that you may be

*able to withstand in the evil day, and having done all,
to stand* [EPHESIANS 6:10-13].

I want to share with you from a testimony of someone who was saved, who had been serving the devil. And when that man gave his testimony, it so challenged me; I did not want to believe it. I had to go ten days before the Lord in fasting, asking Him, *"Lord, is this true?"* It was at that time that the Lord began to teach me what happens in the spiritual realm when we pray.

This man was born after his parents dedicated themselves to Lucifer. When he was still in the womb, they made many rituals dedicating him to serve Lucifer. When he was four years old, he began to exercise his spiritual power. And his parents began fearing him. When he was six years old, his father surrendered him to the witches to go and be trained. And by ten years, he was doing great things in the kingdom of the devil. The normal witches feared him.

He was still a young boy, but he was so terrible in the things he did. He grew up to be a young man in his twenties with so much bloodshed on his hands. He killed at will. He had the ability to go out of his body through transcendental meditation. And he could levitate. Sometimes his body would lift off the ground and stay in the air. And sometimes he could go into a trance, and come out of his body. His body would remain behind and he would go out into the world, called astral-travelling. This guy was used by Satan to break down and destroy so many churches, to destroy so many pastors.

Assigned to Destroy a Church

One day, he was assigned to destroy a church that was so full of prayer. There were many divisions in this church, and many confusions. He began to work on this church. But at that time, the pastor called a fast for the whole church. The church began to fast, and during the fasting, there was a lot of repentance and a lot of reconciliation. The people came together, and they began to pray for the work of the Lord in their midst. They continued interceding and crying to God to have mercy and intervene in their lives. And as they days went by; this man was coming again and again with demon spirits against this church. But there was a word of prophecy that came telling the Christians to rise up and to wage warfare against the powers of darkness that were attacking the church.

So one day, this man leaves his body in his room and goes astral-travelling. He led a mighty force of demonic spirits against this church. Now this is his testimony:

The Yoke Has Been Broken

He was moving in the spirit in the air over the church and they were trying to attack, but there was a covering of light over the church. And suddenly, there was an army of angels that attacked them and there was fighting in the air, and all the demons fled, but he was arrested.

Arrested by whom? The angels! He saw himself being held by about six angels, and they brought him through the roof right before the altar. And there he was. And the people were praying. They were deep in prayer in spiritual warfare, rebuking, breaking and casting out. And the pastor was on the platform leading the prayers and the warfare. The Spirit of the Lord spoke to the pastor, and said, *"The yoke has been broken, and the victim is there before you. Help him through deliverance."* The pastor opened his eyes and saw this young man, who had collapsed there. His body was with him. He was in his body. The young man says he doesn't know how his body joined him; he had left it in his house. But there he was in his body, and he didn't know how he had entered in except the angels had carried him through the roof.

Now these things are difficult to believe, but the pastor silenced the church and told the church what the Lord had told him and asked the young man, *"Who are you?"* The young man was trembling, and the demons began coming out of him. So they prayed for deliverance, and afterwards, he began to share his life. That young man has now come to the Lord and is an evangelist, preaching the Gospel. He is being used by the Lord mightily in setting other people free in the ministry of deliverance.

One night, I went to a dinner, and the sole reason I went was that someone told me about this young man, and I was so curious to see him. So I sat at that dinner and sometime in the evening, this man was given the chance to give his testimony. He talked about many things. Sometimes he cried because of the things he did. And as he finished, he made an appeal.

Teach the People How to Pray

There were so many pastors in that room. And he said, *"I appeal to you, pastors. Please teach the people how to pray."* The people who don't pray can be taken in anything, in anything by the devil, and there are ways that the enemy exploits their lives and their prayers. People who don't know how to pray, they literally pray, and the enemy knows even how to exploit their prayers. We're going to talk about that. And he also said to the pastors, *"Teach the people how to use the spiritual armor that God provides."*

Then he began to give a testimony of how he used to lead expositions into the air. He would go with other satanic agents and lots of demon spirits into the air. It was like a shift, you've got to go and work your shift. So regularly he had a time he had to go and wage war in the heavenlies. And he said that in the heavenlies, in the spiritual realm, if the land is covered under the blanket of darkness, that blanket is so thick, it is like a rock. And it covers the whole area. And these spirits are able to go on top of this as well as below this blanket. And from that level, they influence the events on earth.

Both evil spirits and human agents that are serving the devil and when they leave their shifts they go down on earth at the points of covenant. Even waters or on the land at the points of covenant for refreshing of their spirit. And how do they refresh their spirit? By the sacrifices that people give at these altars. They could be sacrifices in open witchcraft; they could be sacrifices in bloodshed of all types including abortion, including warfare and human sacrifices and animal sacrifices. They could be sacrifices of sexual immorality where people go into sexual perversions and all kinds of promiscuity. And that act services the strength of these powers.

He talked about lots of things, which troubled my mind. He said when they are up there and the Christians begin to pray on earth, the prayers of the Christians appear to them in three forms. All prayers appear like smoke that is rising up into the heavens. That some prayers appear like smoke and they disappear in the air. That the people who pray like that and their prayers disappear, are people who have sin in their lives and are not willing to deal with it. Their prayers are so weak that they disappear in the air.

Prayer Filled with Fire

There are others whose prayers are like smoke that rise up until it reaches this rock, but it does not break through the rock. He said, usually these are those who try to purify themselves, but they lack faith in what they are doing as they pray. And they ignore the other keys to use – areas that they need to put together in prayer. He said that the third type of prayer is like smoke that is filled with fire. As it rises up, it is so hot that as it reaches the rock, the rock begins to melt like wax. It pierces that rock and goes through.

He said many times, people begin to pray and their prayers are like the first type of prayer, but as they continue praying, their prayers change and become like the second prayer. And as they continue praying, suddenly there is fire filling their prayers. And their prayers become so powerful. They pierce through the rock.

Many times, they would notice the prayers of the saints changing and coming very close to the state of fire. They would communicate to other spirits on earth and tell them, *"Distract that person from prayer. Stop them praying. Pull them out."*

Distractions

Many times, so many Christians yield to these distractions. They are pressing through; they are repenting. They are allowing the Word to check their spirit. Faith has been building up. Their prayers are becoming more focused. Then the devil sees their prayers are gaining strength and the distractions begin. Phones ring. Sometimes we are in the middle of very intense prayer, then the phone rings and you go to answer the phone. When you come back, you go back to the beginning. And that's what the devil wants.

Other kinds of distractions come – touching your body, or bringing pain somewhere. Even making you hungry, and you want to fix something to eat. As long as they can get you out of that place, they have defeated you. He said to the pastors, *"Teach people. Set aside some time; not for just some casual kind of praying. They can do that the rest of the day. Once in a day, they should have a time when they are focusing wholeheartedly on God, nothing distracting them. And if people persist in this kind of prayer and allow themselves to be inspired in the Spirit and keep going something happens in the spirit. The fire touches that rock, and it melts."*

That when the melting begins, it is so hot, no demon spirit can stand it. No human spirit can stand it. They all run away. There comes an opening in the spiritual realm. And as soon as it does, all this trouble in prayer stops. The person who is praying feels like prayer is suddenly so smooth, enjoyable, powerful and intense. I have discovered at that moment; we lose consciousness of time and other things. Not that we become disorderly. God takes care of our time. But it is like you lay down everything, and you hook up with God.

Operating Under Open Heavens

This man said that when the prayers go through, from that moment there can be no resistance that can stop him, and the person praying will continue as long as he wants. After he finishes praying, the hole remains open. That when they rise out of their place of prayer, and they walk out, this open hole moves along with them. They are no longer operating under the blanket. They are operating under open heavens. And in that state, the devil cannot do what he wants against them. That the presence of the Lord is like a pillar from heaven resting on their lives. They are protected, and there is so much power inside that pillar that as they move around, that presence touches other people. It discerns what the enemy has done in other people. As they talk to people, those people who are standing with them, come inside this pillar. And as long as they stay inside that pillar, all the bondages of the enemy weaken.

So when these people who have this spiritual breakthrough share Jesus Christ with the sinners, their resistance is low. It is so easy to bring them through. When they pray for the sick or pray about things, the presence, which is there makes all the difference.

He said the devil hates such people. If there are places where prayer is regularly being prayed through like that, the presence comes upon that place and does not leave. So even the people who don't know God, when they come into this place, suddenly all the bondages are weakened. And if someone will minister to them patiently and with love, they can easily be pulled through – not by power nor by might but by the Spirit of God, who is present. If no one bothers about these people, they come into his presence, they feel convicted, they begin to debate whether to yield or not. But if they are not pulled through, when they walk away from that place, bondages get stronger. And the devil tries his best to not let them come back into such an environment.

Satanists Mark and Study Praying People

We were all seated looking at this man. He was telling us the things he used to do and what he used to see. Then he told us what they would do to people who have broken through in prayer. They marked such people; they studied such people. They dug up everything they could find about such people. So they knew their weaknesses. And when someone overcomes them [Satanists] in prayer and breaks through, they communicate with other spirits and say, *"Target him with this and with this and with this. These are his weaknesses."*

So when this person walks out of the prayer closet, the spirit of prayer is upon him, the presence is upon him, his spirit is high, the joy of the Lord is his strength. As he moves the enemy tries to bring things that can distract him from focusing on the Lord. If his weakness is a temper, then the enemy is going to cause people to do things, which can make him really angry. If he is not sensitive to the Holy Spirit, he takes his eyes off the Lord. He gets angry – feeling furious. After a few minutes, he wants to put that behind him and move along in the joy of the Lord, but he doesn't feel it anymore. He tries to feel good again. He doesn't feel any good again. Why? As he yielded to the temptation, they worked hard to close the door upstairs. And once they restore the rock, the presence is cut off.

The person does not cease being a child of God. But that extra anointing on his life, that presence that could do things without manipulating anything, it's just cut off. They seek out the weaknesses. If it is in the temptation to sexuality, the enemy will prepare people, events, something that will suddenly draw out that passion to go towards that temptation. If that man yields to this temptation, and opens up his mind to receive these thoughts, when he is through with everything and wants to move again in the anointing, he discovers it is no longer there.

Maybe you say, *"That's not fair."* Just remember what the Bible says, *"Put on the helmet of salvation. Put on the breastplate of righteousness."* We normally do not see the position, the place of these weapons of warfare. But remember what Jesus told us to pray towards the end of the Lord's prayer, *"Take us not into temptation, but deliver us from the evil one."*

Every time you have a breakthrough in prayer, as you come to the end, remember you are still a weak human being. Remember you have not yet been perfected. Ask the Lord and say *"Lord, I've enjoyed this time of prayer, but when I walk out into this world, lead me not into temptation. Don't allow me to walk into the devil's trap. I know the enemy is setting a trap out there. I don't know what form it is going to take. And I know I am still weak in certain areas. If I am just put in the right place, I will yield to that. Protect me, Lord. When you see me turning that corner where the trap is, just cause me to turn to the other side. Intervene, O Lord. Don't allow me to move by just my own strength and ability. Deliver me from the evil one."*

Thank Him for Everything

God is able to do that. That is why sometimes things happen, all you need to say is, *"Thank you, Jesus!"* That's why Apostle Paul wrote in the book of Thessalonians and said, *"Thank God in everything for that is the will of God in Christ for you."* Some things are not good. They are painful, and we wonder why God would allow it. But if only we knew what He is saving us from, we would thank Him. When we learn to trust the Lord, we just thank Him in everything.

Beloved, I don't know whether to go deeper because I do not want to start something I cannot finish. Let me just try to take one step forward. And this man said that when prayer breaks through like that, the answer will always come. He said he does not know a case where prayer broke through and the answer did not come. He said the answer always came, but in most cases, it would never get to the person who asked. Why? Battle in the heavenlies. He said as long as they succeed in cutting off the open heavens and the rock is restored, they watch this person, they are waiting because they know the answer is definitely coming.

And then this man spoke something that really shook my faith. It is because of the next part he shared that I went into fasting ten days to say, *"Lord, is this true? Can You prove it to me?"*

Pray Clothed in Full Spiritual Armor

This man said that every Christian has got an angel serving that Christian. Now we know the Bible says angels are ministering spirits to us [Heb. 1:14]. He said that when people pray, the answer comes in the hands of the angel. The angel brings the answer like we can read in the book of Daniel. Then he said something really tough. If the one who prays knows the spiritual armor and is clothed with it, the answer comes by an angel who is also clothed in full armor. If the one who prays doesn't care about spiritual armory, their angels come without spiritual armor.

Christians who do not care about what kind of thoughts come into their minds; they don't fight the battle of their minds. Their angels come without the helmet. Whatever spiritual weapon you ignore on earth, the angel doesn't have it as he serves you. In other words, our spiritual armor is not protecting our physical bodies; it's protecting our spiritual exploits.

This man said that when an angel of the Lord comes, the evil spirits will focus and look at him and notice the areas that are not covered, and those are the areas they would attack. If he has no helmet, they would shoot at his head. If he has no breastplate, they would shoot at his chest. If he has no shoes, they would make a fire that he is walking in the fire.

Now I am just repeating what this man said. Actually, we asked him, *"Can angels feel fire?"* And you know what he said? Remember this is a spiritual realm. These are spirits dealing with spirits. The battle is intensive, and when they overpower an angel of God, the first thing they target is the answer he is carrying, and they get that from him. That is what they give through the cults, the witchcraft, and people say, *"I got this because of witchcraft."*

Pray without Ceasing

The Bible says in the book of James, all good things come from God. So where does the devil get the things he gives to his people? Some people who cannot have children, they go to witch doctors and Satanists, and they get pregnant! Who gave them that baby? Is Satan a creator? NO! He steals from those who don't pray to the end. Jesus said, *"Pray without ceasing."* And then He said, *"But when the Son of Man comes, will He find faith?"* Will He find you still there waiting? Or will you have given up and the enemy would steal what you have prayed for?

Then this man said that they are not satisfied with just stealing the answer. They are also interested in detaining the angel. And they start fighting him. And he said sometimes they succeed in holding and binding the angel. When that happens, the Christian is a victim on earth. They can do anything with that Christian because he is left without ministry in the Spirit.

I asked him, *"Do you mean an angel can be held in captivity by demonic forces?"* This man did not know very many scriptures. He was just sharing his experiences. He said they would not hold the angel too long because as other Christians prayed, reinforcement would come, and the angels would go free. If the Christian responsible did not pray through, he remains a captive. Then the enemy sends his own angel as an angel of light to this person, and that is where the deceptions come: False visions and false prophecies. False leadership – leading, guidance in the spirit, making wrong decisions of all types. And many times, this person is open to all kinds of attack and bondages.

I left that dinner so troubled. I asked the Lord, *"Lord, I don't want even to try and believe this."* It removes all my confidence, my security. When I went to seek the Lord, it was ten days. The Lord did two things. He did not only confirm the things I had heard; he opened my mind to see a lot more that this man could not tell us of what happens in the spiritual realm. And two, he led me to see what we are supposed to do as the things are happening so that we are not overcome but that we can overcome. That we need to know three things and really come to terms with these three things:

Three Things to Know for Battle

1. How to operate with the weapons of our warfare. The Bible calls them the armor of God. It is not our armor; it is God's armor. When we use it, we allow God to fight on our behalf.

2. Understand the relationship of the ministering spirits, the angels, to our spiritual lives. And to be sensitive to what is happening in our hearts as a leading to what needs to be

happening in the spirit concerning us. That brings us to the third thing, that is the Holy Spirit.

3. The Holy Spirit is not supposed to come as our servant, serving us and bringing things to us. He does not run to and fro to the Father to tell Him what we need. That is the work of angels. But He stands by our side. Doing what? Guiding us, teaching us, leading us, helping us to pray the right way.

And when these things are happening in the spiritual realm, He tells us. Sometimes He wakes you up in the night and says, *"Pray."* You say, *"No! My time is not yet come."* And He says, *"Pray now!"* Why? He sees what is happening in the spirit. Sometimes He says, *"Tomorrow, fasting!"* You say, *"Oh, no, I'll start on Monday!"* But He understands what is happening in the spiritual realm. We should learn to be sensitive to the Holy Spirit. He guides us in the paths of righteousness.

Dr. John Mulinde, World Trumpet Mission
Prayer Teaching Series:
Opening the Portals of Prayer – Combat in the Heavenlies

LUKE 10:19
Behold, I give you the authority to trample on serpents and scorpions, and over all the power of the enemy, and nothing shall by any means hurt you.

Solemn Assembly

In August 2016, I was called by the Lord to hold a Holy, Solemn Assembly in Ireland. I was to gather as many of His sons and daughters as possible in the land, so that we could come together, humble ourselves, pray, seek His face and turn from our wicked ways, by openly confessing and forsaking our sins. Primarily, by confessing the sins in the Church, that have caused many to become lukewarm. It was a full day of teachings, all to prepare for our time of corporate prayer.

As a ministry, we prepared for months for this meeting, in prayer and with regular fasting. Initially, I was going to fast the seven days leading up to the meeting, breaking it after we ended. But the Lord told me that I was to fast 21 days because it was going to be necessary. We faced much warfare leading up to the meeting, and during the meeting. His counsel is always perfect!

With a small team of volunteers to help facilitate, roles were assigned for the day. At first, I was going to have my ministry partner monitor the room and keep everyone covered in prayer, by walking and praying quietly in the spirit. But at the last minute, the Holy Spirit spoke and said, *"No, she needs to sit in the front row in the chair that is directly in front of you as you speak."*

So I shared her new role, thinking, that if I needed anything she would be right there to help. Where otherwise, if she was walking and praying around the room, I would not be able to easily get her attention, without disrupting the meeting.

The Warfare was Intense

During the morning session, the warfare was intense, but thank God the anointing was flowing strongly as I spoke. It kept me under the Father's hand so strongly that I could not turn to my right or left even if I tried. I say that because while I was speaking, for about a minute, I could hear two women's voices audibly, but low, whispering behind me. The only thing that was behind me was a wall – it did not make sense. At first, I thought it was the worship team and when I glanced their way, they were sitting in their seats.

I carried on and finished that session. The moment I did, it was like a knife was stabbed into my lower back. I knew I was under attack and needed to get to my room as quickly as possible to pray against the attack. For I knew this attack had come to try to destroy our time of prayer, that was to take place after the afternoon teaching that was on prayer.

I could barely walk, and the pain was excruciating. When we got to my room, I asked our team to pray for me, letting them know this attack was from witchcraft. Another woman confirmed that this is what she got too. I knew if this pain did not let up, there would be no way that I would be able to teach, and then lead the time of prayer – to endure through it for another three hours.

After about 20 minutes, I had everyone leave and I sat with the Lord in prayer. I was going to use that time to review my notes, instead, I went into war against this evil assault on my body. Five minutes before our afternoon session was to start the pain greatly let up. The Lord had brought healing, where I could walk and stand without much pain. I was completely healed by the time the last prayer was uttered, and the meeting had ended. There was a powerful breakthrough that came during that time of prayer with relationships being restored, with those who pray for our nation. The enemy surely did not want that to happen!

She Prayed Fervently!

At dinner that night, my ministry partner told me that while I was speaking during the morning session, there were two big, giant brown bugs on the wall directly behind me! And that when she saw them, she started praying fervently for the Lord to protect me from them. For she feared they would fly onto me and disrupt the meeting. She had no idea that I could hear these 'bugs' voices, but I did not see them, for I did not turn around to see where the voices were coming from. If I had, it surely would have taken me off guard, and would have stopped the anointing from flowing and the words that needed to be spoken from being heard.

As soon as she told me this, I knew these 'bugs' were really witches that had transformed themselves into these 'giant bugs' to come to destroy God's plans for us as a people, tribe, tongue and nation that day. I marveled at the wisdom of God and His faithfulness to protect us, by having her sit directly in front of me. For if she had not, only God knows what the outcome would have been! It was also the source of the physical attack on me. Not just by these 'bugs,' but by others who were in our midst, wolves in sheep's clothing. I could then understand why the Lord told me 21-days of fasting was going to be necessary.

Demons Have Power to Transform

For those who may struggle with what I share, let me say that there is a man by the name of Bishop Samuel Vagalas Kanco, who has first-hand experience in what I experienced, prior to my ever hearing about him. I highly recommend his book, *The Witch Doctor and The Man City Under The Sea.*[24] He goes into great detail, revealing the depth of evil of witchcraft that takes place in churches. Why? Because the Lord wants His people not to be deceived, but instead to be prepared and armed. Before getting saved and going on to have a powerful deliverance ministry, Bishop Kanco was a fourth-generation witchdoctor. From before his birth he was indoctrinated with the vilest occultic rituals, that empower demons to work in one's life.

In his book, he shares how when he was young, Satan had given him the power to change into five different animals. He shared that a demon told him how that demon had the power to affect transformations with humans – changing humans to animals and vice versus. That he had the power to fly and go through walls with these new body forms. He was taught as a child how to change a lizard into a crocodile, frog or fly. Flies were sent to put sickness on people by biting them or leaving poison or witchcraft behind in their food. He learned how other sorcerers were changed into flies to be carried on people's shoulders.[25] If you still doubt such things can take place, remember that Satan transformed himself into a serpent and because of it, he was able to deceive Eve.

GENESIS 3:13 AMP.
And the Lord God said to the woman, what is this you have done? And the woman said, the serpent beguiled (cheated, outwitted, and deceived) me, and I ate.

These dark occultic powers are real. They are very active today in the Church, targeting believers, and their goal is to distract and destroy the plans of God in our lives. Paul speaks of this to the Corinthians, fearing they would be beguiled like Eve and follow another 'Jesus' or a different spirit, and fall away from pure devotion to Christ.

> **2 Corinthians 11:3-4 AMP.**
> *But [now] I am fearful, lest that even as the serpent beguiled Eve by his cunning, so your minds may be corrupted and seduced from wholehearted and sincere and pure devotion to Christ. For [you seem readily to endure it] if a man comes and preaches another Jesus than the One we preached, or if you receive a different spirit from the [Spirit] you [once] received or a different gospel from the one you [then] received and welcomed; you tolerate [all that] well enough!*

Satan is real. He hides in the shadows, clothed in fear, confusion and division. He works overtime to destroy what God wants to do in and though us, and especially through our prayer life. Angels, demons, fallen angels – spiritual warfare all exist. But we do not need to live in fear of Satan's realm of darkness. God has given us everything that we need to overcome it His way – the blood of the Lamb, the Word and His Holy Spirit to lead and guide us into all truth. All these were given to us, so that we would trample every serpent, scorpion and demonic force under the souls of our feet! AMEN!

CHAPTER 7

UNHOLY ALLIANCES

And many of those who had practiced curious, magical arts collected their books and [throwing them, book after book, on the pile] burned them in the sight of everybody. When they counted the value of them, they found it amounted to 50,000 pieces of silver [Acts 19:19 Amp].

In Opening Portals of Prayer, we saw how a former Satanist worked his black magic on Christians. How he often astral-travelled to destroy churches, and the prayer that was taking place in those places of worship, by causing division and confusion. He came to their meetings in spirit form so no one with their natural eyes could see what he was doing. And that it was during a time of corporate fasting and prayer, where the whole church had humbled themselves confessing their sins, that caused his wicked works to be exposed to the pastor. They were then able to destroy his works against them through prayer, and he got saved and delivered.

Unholy Alliances Give the Enemy Legal Access

One of the main reasons this former Satanist was able to have access to so many Christians is because of the many unholy alliances that believers have in their lives. When we have unholy alliances, it gives the enemy legal access to work his evil powers against us. We see that in Acts chapter 19 when some of the Jewish exorcists – the sons of Sceva, attempted to use the name of Jesus to deliver some men who were under the influence of evil spirits. Because of their unholy alliances, though, the demons did not recognise Jesus in them, and overpowered and wounded them – causing them to flee.

Acts 19:13-16

Then some of the itinerant Jewish exorcists took it upon themselves to call the name of the Lord Jesus over those who had evil spirits, saying, "We exorcise you by the Jesus whom Paul preaches." Also there were seven sons of Sceva, a Jewish chief priest, who did so. And the evil spirit answered and said, "Jesus I know, and Paul I know; but who are you?" Then the man in whom the evil spirit was leaped on them, overpowered them, and prevailed against them, so that they fled out of that house naked and wounded.

In Paul's day, Ephesus, now modern-day Turkey, was known for its occultic practices and rituals. Ephesus was home to the Temple of Artemis that was built and dedicated to the Greek deity Artemis. Artemis was goddess over the hunt, the moon and chastity. The Greeks highly revered this pagan deity.

So, right after the sons of Sceva were beaten by the evil spirits, the fear of the Lord fell upon the Jews and Greeks, causing many to be saved who then burned all their occultic books.

Acts 19:17-19

This became known both to all Jews and Greeks dwelling in Ephesus; and fear fell on them all, and the name of the Lord Jesus was magnified. And many who had believed came confessing and telling their deeds. Also, many of those who had practiced magic brought their books together and burned them in the sight of all. And they counted up the value of them, and it totaled fifty thousand pieces of silver.

Harry Potter

Today, we need to see a lot of burning of occultic books and DVDs that have made their way into the Church, and into our Christian homes. Harry Potter, Chronicles of Narnia and Lord of the Rings – just to name a few. They are saturated in witchcraft, wizardry and divination, all promoting Satan's kingdom of darkness. They do not glorify the Lord Jesus Christ.

I believe the Harry Potter books are more obvious to those who are living a consecrated and holy life unto the Lord, as occultic. Yet, there are many in the Church today who read these books, and flock to see these movies, and then wonder why their lives and others are in such a mess. Many have children who are suicidal, addicted to alcohol and drugs, and becoming more rebellious with every passing day. Many have marriages falling apart. Pornography continues to increase in our homes, taking many souls captive. And, sadly, we pay a lot of money to promote this evil in our lives!

J.K. Rowling, the author of the Harry Potter series, is the second highest paid author in the world. At one time she was a billionaire from the sales of her witchcraft-promoting books, Wizarding World at Universal Studios, and Broadway's *Harry Potter and the Cursed Child* play. As of 2020, Forbes estimates her current net worth to have dropped to $60 million.[26] That is a lot of money being sowed into promoting the 'craft.'

Rowling distances herself from the reports that she is a witch and that she has very little knowledge of the craft. In Reuters, she was quoted on July 17, 2000 saying, *"The character of Harry just strolled into my head ... I really did feel he was someone who walked up and introduced himself to my mind's eye."*[27] Her childhood friend, Ian Potter, remembers her dressing up as a witch all the time. Her younger sister Vikki said, *"Our favorite thing was to dress up as witches. We used to dress up and play witch all the time. My brother would dress up as a wizard. Joanne was always reading witchcraft stories to us. We would make secret potions for her. She would always send us off to get twigs for the potions."*[28]

During a 1999 radio interview, Rowling reveals while writing her books she studied mythology, witchcraft and the exact words used in witches' spells.[29] She had graduated earlier from a course in mythological studies at Exeter University. And *"She has an extremely well-developed and sophisticated knowledge of the occult world, its legends, history and nuances."*[30]

How Can Light Have Fellowship with Darkness?

So, how can the *Hogwarts School of Witchcraft and Wizardry* or any of J.K. Rowling's other witchcraft books have any place in our lives, if we say we are a Christian and a follower of Jesus? How can Light have anything to do with darkness? Her teachings, in her books on life after death in the form of reincarnation and communicating with the dead, are nothing less than calling up demons who come as familiar spirits, masquerading behind the face of departed ones. Her books from beginning to end are full of magic, sorcery and divination of the evilest kind. Why would we want anything to do with them, or let our children have access to them?

> **2 CORINTHIANS 6:14 AMP**
> *Do not be unequally yoked with unbelievers [do not make mismated alliances with them or come under a different yoke with them, inconsistent with your faith]. For what partnership have right living and right standing with God with iniquity and lawlessness? Or how can light have fellowship with darkness?*

Rowling teaches that death is to be desired. That it is the entrance to the next great adventure.[31] In a 2004 interview, Rowling shares that the killing curse 'avada kedavra' used in her books, comes from the word abracadabra.[32] Abracadabra is from the Chaldean word 'abbada ke dabra' which means 'perish like the word.' Her teachings are void of life, and opposite to the life and teachings of our Savior and Redeemer, the Author and Giver of life – the Lord Jesus Christ!

In Jesus, we do not desire death, but seek the abundant life that can only be found in Him. There is nothing dark or dead about Jesus! And He desires that none should perish, but we would all turn back to Him in repentance.

The Chronicles of Narnia

I believe it is easier to see the darkness to Rowling's writings, but not as easily when it comes to C.S. Lewis' and J.R.R. Tolkien's writings for many Christians. In particular, *The Chronicles of Narnia: The Lion, the Witch and the Wardrobe* and *The Lord of the Rings* trilogy, respectively.

Most would believe these writings are a form of 'symbolism' displaying the forces of good and evil, where good must triumph over evil. That they are harmless to our souls, and are actually good for us. Mainstream Christianity esteems C.S. Lewis as a great Christian writer, with profound teachings of 'Christianity' in his books. His books can be found in just about every Christian bookstore. They can also be found in occult bookstores everywhere!

Pastor David J. Meyer, a former witch and occultist, who had practiced astrology, palmistry, and numerology among other devices of the craft, shares valuable insight into these writings. In tracts he has written, he reveals the dark side of both authors, and the foundation of their writings.

He states that the works of C.S. Lewis are required reading by neophyte witches. This includes *The Chronicles of Narnia*, because it teaches neophyte, or new witches, the basic mindset of the craft. He shares that the release date of the movie – December 9th, was the 13th day before the witches' quarter-sabat of Yule. The full cold moon is midway between the release date and the sabat of Yule. The waxing moon is also directly on the equinox on the release date of the movie. This is far too precisely occultic to be coincidental, and those behind the scenes for making the decision for when this movie would release, would have knowledge from upper-level witches regarding the perfect day to have the *Chronicles of Narnia* open.

Clive Staples Lewis was a professor at Oxford University in England where he was supposedly converted to 'Christianity' by another Oxford professor named J.R.R. Tolkien. Tolkien often referred to Lewis as a 'reluctant Christian.' Tolkien was a Roman Catholic in doctrine.

Not Sunday School Material!

The Narnian Chronicle is one of clandestine occult mysticism. It is not Sunday School material unless your Sunday School is a defacto witch coven. The story involves a child, Lucy, who hides in a wardrobe while playing a game, and suddenly finds herself transported to another world unlike her own. She soon finds herself having tea with a faun.

In witchcraft and ancient Roman pagan mythology, a faun is any of a group of rural deities, which have the bodies of men and the horns, ears, tails, and legs of a goat. The Roman god Faunus was also the god of nature and fertility and was connected to sexual lust. This same strange land the little girl finds herself in is also populated by gods and goddesses; such as Bacchus, the god of drunken orgies, and the Maenads, who were frenzied women driven to madness in the orgiastic cult of Bacchus.

The main character is a lion named Aslan, which is the Turkish word for lion. Aslan is the character that Christians say is the Christ figure, but witches know him to be Lucifer. Aslan, appears in all seven of the books. He is esteemed to be the 'Christ figure' by many Christians. With that in mind, consider the following quotes from *The Chronicles of Narnia*:

"The crowd and dance round Aslan grew so thick and rapid that Lucy was confused. She never saw where certain other people came from who were soon capering among the trees. One was a youth, dressed only in a fawn skin, with vine leaves wreathed in his curly hair. His face would have been almost too pretty for a boy's, if it had not looked so extremely wild.

You felt, as Edmund said when he saw him a few days later, 'There's a chap who might do anything, absolutely anything.' He seemed to have a great many names – Bromios, Bassareus, and the Ram were three of them. There were a lot of girls with him, as wild as he. There was even, unexpectedly, someone on a donkey. And everybody was laughing: and everyone was shouting out, 'EUAN, EUAN, EU-oi-oi-oi.'"

Those strange words EUAN, EUAN, EU-oi-oi-oi are an ancient witches' chant used to invoke the power and presence of the god of drunkenness and addiction, who is named Bacchus.

Witches Sabat of Midsummer

It gets worse as the witchcraft increases and becomes more obvious, consider the following:

"'What is it Aslan?' said Lucy, her eyes dancing and her feet wanting to dance. 'Come children', said he. 'Ride on my back today.' 'Oh lovely!' cried Lucy, and both girls climbed onto the warm golden back as they had done no one knew how many years before. Then the whole party moved off – Aslan leading. Bacchus and his Maenads leaping, rushing and turning somersaults, the beasts brushing round them, and Silenus and his donkey bringing up the rear... Then three or four Red Dwarfs came forward with their tinder boxes and set light to the pile, which first crackled, and then blazed, and finally roared as a woodland bonfire on midsummer night ought to do. And every-one sat down in a wide circle around it. Then Bacchus and Silenus and the Maenads began a dance, far wilder than the dance of the trees, not merely a dance for fun and beauty (though it was that too), but a magic dance of plenty, and where their hands touched, and where their feet fell, the feast came into existence. Sides of roasted meat that filled the grove with delicious smell, and wheaten cakes and oaten cakes..."

The above describes a witches' sabat of Midsummer or the Summer Solstice, and it is described in perfect detail.

In Lewis' book, *The World's Last Night and Other Essays* on pages 98-99, he said, *"Assuredly, I say to you, this generation will by no means pass away till all these things take place...certainly the most embarrassing verse in the Bible. The one exhibition of error and the one confession of ignorance grow side by side. That they stood thus in the mouth of Jesus himself and were not merely placed thus by the reporter, we surely need not doubt... The facts, then, are these: that Jesus professed himself (in some sense) ignorant, and within a moment showed that he really was so."* In *Reflections on the Psalms*, page 129, Lewis wrote, *"... as I believe, Christ... fulfilled both paganism and Judaism."*

The above statements and quotes were taken from Pastor David J. Myer's tract, *The Witchcraft of the Narnia Chronicles.*[33]

The Lord of the Rings

The Lord of the Rings trilogy was written by J.R.R. Tolkien and first published in the 1950's. During the explosion of the 60's rock music scene, over 100 million copies were sold. These books greatly fueled the spiritual revolution and opened the door for witchcraft to seize our world. All to prepare the way for a new world order in a new Aquarian age.

Pastor David J. Meyer, whose life at one time was very much a part of the world that J.R.R. Tolkien portrays in *The Lord of the Rings* trilogy, shares that witches and Satanists are not the same thing. Witches do not believe in Satan. The first thing a neophyte or beginner witch is taught is that there is a 'force.' The 'force' has two sides and can be controlled by magic spells, words, potions, incantations, rope magic, rings, amulets, and so on. Witches believe that there is good witchcraft and bad witchcraft, and the good always triumphs over evil! Witches also teach that battles are fought in the Middle Earth and in the astral plane causing upheavals both above and below. Thus, witches emphasise that good must triumph over evil, but it is all witchcraft.

Many Christians and leaders, defend such works as *Harry Potter*, *The Lord of the Rings*, and *The Narnia Chronicles*. They say the same things that initiated coven witches say, *"That good triumphs over evil!"* It is all witchcraft, and the good that these Christians are defending is witchcraft as forbidden in Deuteronomy 18:9-14.

The Lord of the Rings trilogy was the work of John Ronald Reuel Tolkien, who did his writing during the midnight hours. He worked for 12 years and released his story in the 13th year. Tolkien became known as the 'Master of the Middle Earth.' This was a land inhabited by hobbits, elves, mortal men, wizards, dwarves and orcs or grotesque goblins. The hero of the story is a hobbit or halfling only 3 ½ feet tall named Frodo Baggins. Frodo has pointed ears and furry feet and carries a cursed object with him. The cursed object is a golden ring invested with terrible powers that must be destroyed by casting it into a fiery abyss at a great distance. If Frodo would fail, the ring would fall into the hands of an evil wizard called Sauron, and the entire world would pass into eternal darkness under the dark lord. Sauron's world is a land of shadows called Mordor. The ring has an inscription on which is written a message in the witchcraft language of runes.

Runes Are Real

These runes are real and used in the occult. Pastor Meyer reveals the meaning of the runes, and he notes that a former United States President wore an exact replica of this ring. The runes on the ring are interpreted as follows: *"One ring to rule them all, one ring to find them, one ring to bring them all and in the darkness bind them."*

J.R.R. Tolkien once said, *"I desired dragons with a profound desire."* He spoke German, French, Latin, and flawless classical Greek. In speech, he would sometimes break out in Gothic, an ancient form of German. He would also speak medieval Welsh and Anglo-Saxon. Tolkien developed a new language called Elvish. He said that the entire story of *The Lord of the Rings* came to him as a result of the new language that he invented.

He was a professor at Oxford University while the story of elves, wizards, trolls, and hobbits poured into his mind. While it became a manuscript under his pen, he said, *"My work has escaped from my control, I have produced a monster."* Tolkien, a devout Catholic and 'Master of Middle Earth,' converted his colleague C.S. Lewis and spent much time with him at the Oxford pub. They claimed to have 'kindred spirits.'

There is much blasphemy in Tolkien's works, such as the death and resurrection of the wizard Gandalf, who falls into the pit and descends into hell but comes back transformed and stronger than ever. Deceived Christians say that this 'good wizard' is a type of Christ! Tolkien even translated the Lord's Prayer into the Elvish language!

Pastor Meyer states that *The Lord of the Rings* trilogy comes from the pits of hell and is a clever instructional course in witchcraft disguised as fantasy and entertainment. Part one, *The Fellowship of the Ring*, was released as a movie on December 19, 2001. Shortly after the two towers of the World Trade Center came down, part two, *The Two Towers*, was released on December 18, 2002. Part three, *The Return of the King*, was released December 17, 2003. All three movies were released at the time of the witchcraft sabat of Yule!

Pastor Meyer's prayer, *"As a preacher of the true Gospel, is Christians will come fully awake. We do not find the saving Gospel in the Middle Earth with wizards, hobbits, and elves. We find the Gospel only in the Bible and through the blood of our Savior Jesus."*

The above statements and quotes were taken from Pastor David J. Myer's tract, *A Former Witch Looks at the Lord of the Rings.*[34]

Demons Can Keep Us Spellbound

Beloved, these are only a few of the occultic books that need to be burned if a part of our homes, churches or ministries. For every time we pick up one of these books, or watch one of these movies, we are entering into unholy alliances and inviting demons to influence our lives and those around us. They are keeping us spellbound, wanting us to miss God's plans for us.

For those who may say, it is "harmless," or "I am covered under the blood of the Lamb," we need to know that real curses and demons are attached to these books, to influence those who read them. By bringing them into our lives, we invite and open the door for demons to dwell in our midst. These writings were not meant for good. The blood of the Lamb can only protect us when we walk in obedience to His Word, and when we repent for sin in our lives.

By having these books in our lives, we create an open portal of an evil kind that gives Satan, and his hordes of demons, freedom to access and destroy our lives. It is not a light matter and too many in the Church today have made it a light matter. Many hold tightly to these occultic books, while holding loosely to the Word of God. Many Christians are being pulled into the realm of the occult, because they are ignorant of Satan's devices.[35]

If you are one such person, please I beg you – do not harden your heart to these words! Instead, pray, seek His face and with a humble heart, remove these books from your home – from your church! Turn to the Lord in repentance. Ask Him to forgive you for allowing the occult to gain entrance into your life and defile your soul – your relationships. He is merciful – so patient with us and more than willing to forgive, when we ask. He is not looking to shame or condemn us, but wants to cleanse us and set us free! When you are done, ask for the blood of the Lamb to cleanse you from every way these occultic and unholy alliances have polluted and defiled your mind, will, emotions and intellect – your children, your marriage, the sheep you have been entrusted to steward into His holy ways. Then receive His love and forgiveness, knowing He is fighting for you and not against you!

Rebellion the Sin of Witchcraft

There are some who have no issues in getting rid of these books, but have loved ones in their household who refuse to do so. It has not been easy to convince them of the harm these books are doing in their lives. This stronghold can be so great in a person who is not truly following the Lord – they may be in word, but not in action. For them to be able to receive the truth that would cause them to want to get rid of these books, will not happen without a major battle in the spirit realm. Remember, the sin of witchcraft is rebellion, and stubbornness the sin of idolatry. It is why the battle can be so great. For those are just two of the demons that we invite to rule over our souls, the eyes of our heart's understanding, when we partake in the occult, whether we know it or not. Often, it will take fasting and prayer to break the stronghold.

1 Samuel 15:23

For rebellion is as the sin of witchcraft, and stubbornness is as iniquity and idolatry. Because you have rejected the word of the Lord, He also has rejected you from being king."

Accountability

If your children have these books, as their parent and the authority of your household, it is your responsibility to purge the evil that is in your midst. Do it only in love, in humility and explain why they must be removed using the Word of God as your foundation. But do not leave it up for debate. The Lord holds parents accountable for what they allow into their children's lives until they reach the age of accountability, that most agree is the age of thirteen. At the same time, the Lord holds all heads of household accountable for what they allow into their homes regardless of age. So, if you have older children living with you, it is still your responsibility to be the gate keeper for what comes in and out of your household, for He has given you the authority to rule your home according to His holy, righteous ways.

Once the books have been removed, we would then want to confess and repent of the sin of witchcraft, along with the sins of rebellion and idolatry, whether it was willful or out of ignorance on our part, by reading and promoting these books. We would then want to break off all the curses and spells that have been placed upon our lives because of our ties with them. These curses and spells can only be broken once we have repented and no longer partake in it.

If at all possible, then burn the books, if you have a safe means to do so. If not, I recommend putting them in the unrecyclable garbage – not the recyclable. Why? So those spells and curses will not be ground up to be used in future matter – we want to end the cycle of curses and evil, not keep it going!

When we repent and remove these occultic books from our midst, we can be assured the Word of the Lord will grow greatly and prevail in our lives, families, churches and ministries! We have the same hope and promise for that good fruit to come forth, that the Jews and the Greeks experienced in Acts chapter 19, right after they burned all their occultic books.

Acts 19:20
So the word of the Lord grew mightily and prevailed.

Halloween

Many Christians will have nothing to do with Halloween, yet there are many that believe it is harmless and think there is nothing wrong it. Then there are those in the middle. Some churches will have a 'harvest party' on that night, substituting the demonic costumes with Bible characters. They will play games and encourage families to come, as a good way to spend that night, calling evil now good.

Halloween is pagan and occultic to the very core of its Druid origins. It is the most wicked night on the occultists' calendar, where witches and Satanists offer animal and human blood sacrifices to Satan. It could be described as Satan's birthday, if he had such a thing. There is nothing good or redemptive about Halloween, other than the day it will be utterly destroyed in the Millennium Reign, when the Lord returns with His Bride to rule and reign over the nations for 1,000 years. The Church and too many believers try to spiritualise away the evil roots of Halloween, along with all the other pagan days they celebrate, thinking that because they are a child of Christ, those evil roots cannot affect them. They could not be more deceived.

Halloween originated in Europe. History shows that Ireland is where it primarily got its dark beginnings, from the Druids who were Celtic priests. Their celebration on this night was of everything wicked, evil and dead, and known as the 'Festival of Samhain' or 'Feast of the Dead.' Samhain was known as the lord of the dead, and is the demonic spirit that is worshipped during this celebration. It is why there is an emphasis on death symbols: coffins, tombstones, skulls, skeletons, ghosts and graveyards. The Festival of Samhain marked the end of the Celtic year and the beginning of the new one. As such, it can be seen to the equivalent of New Year's Eve.[36]

All Saints Day

Halloween was brought into the Church through the Roman Catholic Church in the early AD 700's when they changed the name to 'All Hallow's Day' which means 'All Saints Day.' Which takes place on November 1st. On 'Hallow's Eve,' the evening before 'Hallow's Day,' is October 31st or known as 'Hallow'en, Hallow evening, or Halloween.'[37]

So, as a Christian, should we partake in pagan customs and rituals of ancient people and 'christianise' them? Moses and Jeremiah say that we are not to learn after the abominations of those nations, and to not learn the way of the heathen.

> **Deuteronomy 18:9**
> *When you come into the land which the Lord your God is giving you, you shall not learn to follow the abominations of those nations.*

> **Jeremiah 10:2-3**
> *Thus says the Lord: "Do not learn the way of the Gentiles; Do not be dismayed at the signs of heaven, For the Gentiles are dismayed at them. **For the customs of the peoples are futile;***

Isaiah further spoke about this in chapter 5:

Isaiah 5:20

Woe to those who call evil good, and good evil; Who put darkness for light, and light for darkness; Who put bitter for sweet, and sweet for bitter!

And Paul says we are to have no fellowship with the unfruitful works of darkness, but rather expose them!

Ephesians 5:11

And have no fellowship with the unfruitful works of darkness, but rather expose them.

When Christians partake in Halloween, it sends a message to not just our children but the world around us that witchcraft, Satanism and the occult are fun, entertaining and harmless. It gives the false impression that what is actually lethal to our souls is harmless. It is the spiritual equivalent of painting a loaded gun to look like a toy and then giving it to a child to play with![38]

Witches and Warlocks in the Church

In October 2018, while doing some meetings in the North of Ireland, I met with an intercessor who had the gift of discernment. We discussed many things causing the topic to move to witchcraft. I shared how witches and warlocks have infiltrated the Church, sharing my own experiences of how they can mask themselves to look and sound like a 'Christian.'

This woman then had a warning for me about a person we had met in Dublin months prior, telling me that I needed to be careful. I was greatly troubled by what she shared, and it was exactly what we had been talking about – wolves in sheep's clothing. I sought the Lord for weeks, needing to know if what had been spoken was truth or not. I did not have any reason to believe she was lying – in fact, the opposite. When she spoke, my spirit witnessed to what was being said. I had seen signs over the months within the person in question and had questioned the Lord a few times, but I had always pushed it aside, feeling horrible for thinking this person was evil.

Bewitched and Beguiled Again!

I did not connect the dots until this meeting, but I still needed to hear from the Lord myself before I could come to any final conclusion. Obviously, someone was lying to me, and I needed to know who! If what she said was true, then I had been bewitched and beguiled again! And, not only myself, but many intercessors for this person was connected.

We continued to do our meetings in the North. During this time, I had been called to a 12-day fast that was to end once the meetings were complete. I had been warned by the Lord that the warfare was going to be great. It was my first time to the North, and I had no idea how dark it was – meaning full of witchcraft, until we arrived in Letterkenny, Co. Donegal. We had an offer to stay at a B&B that was owned by believers. It sounded good! But for a couple of reasons it was not working out. When seeking His counsel if we were to stay there, the Lord told me, *"No, that spells and curses had been put on that place and we were not to stay there, but in the hotel where the meetings were being held."*

It was not made known to me who had put the spells or curses on this property, the owners or others – just that the spells and curses existed and we were not to stay there. I did not need to know more for the Lord had answered my prayer whether or not we were to stay there. I have learned early on to just obey the voice of the Lord and not ask questions, that I do not need to know the details, or why He says something. What is important is that we just obey and not reason it away with our finite thinking.

Taxi Driver Encounter

After the Letterkenny meeting, we traveled to Derry and the darkness increased greatly! Once settled into my hotel room, I got a taxi into Derry town centre to get some items that I needed. While waiting in the queue for my return taxi, I watched the flow of traffic. All taxis were coming from one direction. When it was my turn, the taxi that I was to get into came from the opposite way. I had a check in my spirit as I walked over to the car, saying, *"This is going to be interesting, Lord."* When I went to grab the door handle to get into the back seat, I found none. There was no door handle to grab, only one for the front passenger seat.

I made a mental note, thinking this is odd, a two-door taxi – how that would limit their passenger load and income greatly. When I opened the door, I went to get into the back seat. But there was no lever to pull the seat forward. Even odder, the back-seat area was completely dark – I could not see any back seats! I know that may sound odd, but I am not exaggerating. I thought, *"Okay, Lord, this is going to be really interesting."*

When the driver asked me what I was doing in Derry, our conversation turned to the Lord, after sharing we were there to do a prayer meeting. He then said, *"I am going to play the 'devil's advocate.' Is there a heaven or a hell?"* The moment he said that, I had another check in my spirit of a serious nature. I knew this was not going to be any ordinary conversation.

I replied, *"Both. Why do you ask? Do you want to know Jesus – eternity is a really long time."* He agreed saying, *"Yes, eternity is a really long time. Who created hell?"* I explained God, but it was originally created for Satan and the fallen angels who rebelled against Him. The man could not accept that and got very angry, and started yelling. He said, *"God knows everything, He knew Satan would rebel. That the angels would rebel. So why then did He create hell?"* I tried to explain that we have a free will. This made him angrier! He did not believe we have a free will. He said, *"God is so hateful, because He knew I would fall and created hell."*

Our Free Will

I tried to share again, that we get to decide who we will serve, who we will obey. That we have a free will and He is a good God all the time, but He will never go against our free will. The man became more rageful, saying, *"God knows everything – He knew that a billion years ago this day would come when you would get into this taxi."* I agreed, saying, *"Yes, He knows all things – He knew this would happen."* He then said more than once, *"If I drive this car into that wall right now, it is not my free will because God knows everything that will happen."* I said, *"Yes, you could drive this car into the wall right now, but that would be your choice – your free will."* He only got angrier and yelled more, if possible! I was truly trying to help him understand we have free will.

After continuing to yell at me about how evil God was, not letting me say anymore, I finally interrupted him asking, *"Are you interested at all in what I have to say, or do you just want to yell at me the whole time?"* He became silent. I shared how God created us a spirit-being with a free will. That He is a God of relationship, therefore He will never force Himself upon us. That we get to decide to do good or evil, it is up to us. That He sends no one to hell – we are the ones that will send ourselves to hell, if we choose to disobey Him and His Word.

That was all I could say, for he continued to yell at me, until we got to the hotel. When I got out of the car, I blessed him, and told him that I pray the Lord Jesus would reveal Himself and His love to him. With piercing dark eyes, he looked at me and with such hate said, *"I believe in religion, I just do not believe in God."*

During this encounter, I never once had fear and was at perfect peace, even when this man threatened a few times to drive the car into the wall. For he really did want to kill me. But I was in the centre of the Father's will and it was not my time to die, therefore he could not. But I did not understand what the Lord had allowed me to walk through, and why? That night I asked, *"Lord, what was all that about?"*

The following day, while waiting on the Lord, He shared the following word:

Many Oppose My Light

"Many oppose My Light – they love the darkness that is in them and around them. They love what makes them comfortable – not what makes them uncomfortable. Those who choose to stay comfortable – holding onto darkness, when My Light comes making them uncomfortable will miss Me. You are that light I have sent – to shine My Light into their dark souls, giving them an opportunity to choose My ways, to choose to abandon what makes their souls – their flesh feel good.

It is true this woman [one I had been warned about] is not for you. Her motives have been impure towards you from the beginning. It is wise to be guarded. I want you to do the meeting. I will gather out of this dark place those who will follow Me – want My Light. You will not miss the darkness in this woman this time. I will make it clear to you, that this will not be a stumbling block to you but a stepping-stone. You discerned correctly that woman [another woman in her circle] has been bewitched, charmed and seduced by this relationship. Keep praying for her to be free from these influences.

You were weak, under many attacks, many disappointments – much rejection [from others] – this is why you did not fully see the danger in this person. At one time, more than once you questioned if things were right, you became unguarded. Daughter I know this is all troubling you greatly now – feeling sick about what I AM saying. You have asked to know – I do not desire to let this be hidden from you. My daughter was correct and sent to help you. The battle has been fierce against you. I AM fighting for you! Keep releasing My Light. Keep worshipping Me. My Light is pushing back the darkness.

Satan's plans, like yesterday, will fail [taxi driver]. Fear not those who come to destroy you as you witnessed yesterday. No darkness can stand against My Light. Yes, that man was sent to destroy you. It was a divine setup by Satan himself who sent one of his chief warlocks to destroy you. I wanted you to experience this first hand. It is something I will have you share. It is a sobering time for My church who is asleep, bewitched, seduced and beguiled by sorcery.

I did not want you to stay at that B&B. Many spells and curses have been placed upon that land trapping and snaring many of My people – causing them to be blinded to truth – to the plans I have for them.

You are thinking about the 'dog poo' that was in My daughter's house after that woman got up to go to bed, that it was on the carpet, where she was sitting. Two things: One, it was Satan's way of trying to pollute the atmosphere – affect My daughter. Two, it was a sign – a mark left behind marking this woman as unclean. When you get back, I want you both to [spiritually] cleanse her house. You have authority over this evil – the witchcraft. I want you to use My Sword – the sword I have given you – truth, to cut its head off. Do not hesitate [to cut it off], and because you do [cut it off] many will come out of the darkness and into My Light.

Stay vigilant in prayer. Grow weary and faint not knowing in due season you shall reap a great reward. In the midst of adversity, I will show Myself strong on behalf of those who walk upright before Me. Fear not Tracy, fear not – I AM with you."

Unclean Imprint

You may wonder about the reference to the 'dog poo.' It was one of the signs that caused me to question the motives of this woman months earlier. While this woman was at a friend's home, she discovered dog poo on her carpet, where this woman had been sitting. It was in just one place, not a track of it, like if it had been on your shoe and you did not know – you would leave a trail.

Her family did not own a dog. They had traveled in her car together, prior to entering her home. If it had come from their travels, it would have been on the car floor mat, but there was none. The only place this 'unclean imprint' had been left was in the house, where she sat.

When my friend shared this, it got my attention, as we face constant warfare being a prayer ministry. My friend had discerned it was of the enemy trying to affect her, and the prayer meetings we were doing, but she did not connect it directly to that woman. Until several weeks later, during her time of prayer, she had a vision and saw this woman lighting a candle with a rageful look on her face.

Interesting enough, I found out months after these encounters, that Derry, Co. Derry, was known to be the Halloween 'capital' or 'centre' of Ireland for the past 10 years, at that time. Beloved, these powers are real and they come to destroy. As a believer, who has been bought by the blood of the Lamb, we do not have the right to partake in any wicked traditions of man that have to do with Halloween. If we do, we are playing with fire. And if we do not repent, we will not only be led astray, but will get burned!

ROMANS 13:12
The night is far spent, the day is at hand. Therefore let us cast off the works of darkness, and let us put on the armor of light.

Púca Festival, Ireland 2019

In January 2019, the Irish Government announced Fáilte Ireland was going to spend €4 million on a new 'large-scale international festival' to attract thousands of visitors to Ireland for Halloween. They wanted to create a new festival that will "celebrate Ireland as the original home of Halloween, which began as the ancient tradition of Samhain – the ancient New Year." Their plan is to attract 100,000 visitors to the festival as part of Ireland's Ancient East with plans to generate €12 million in tourism revenue.

Fáilte Ireland had multiple goals for the festival. To lure people to Ireland, under the guise of tourism, to partake in the Samhain – Halloween festival. This festival included the curation and delivery of "an authentic, high-quality festival that is distinctive from other Halloween events in an exceptionally rich and historic setting, that will become a 'bucket-list cultural experience' that will motivate people to travel from around the world to visit."

There was a display of outdoor night-time installation that symbolised the ancient ritual of the lighting of the first fires in the surrounding hills, with specific consideration given to the Hill of Ward and the Hill of Tara. It is believed that the Festival of Samhain first originated at the top of the Hill of Ward, or Tlachtga, near Athboy in Co. Meath. The installation goal was to motivate significant numbers of visitors to come to it, as well for it to be captured and shared globally. The programme was to include existing festivals such as the *Flame of Samhain Festival* in Athboy and the *Spirits of Meath Festival*.

Púca Festival was the name given to this new festival. Púca is a Celtic folklore character associated with Samhain, who is known as the lord of darkness and the lord of death. It was three days of lights and music, from October 31 – November 2, 2019. It opened with a 'Samhain procession and arrival of the spirits' that commemorated Samhain and the beginning of the darker half of the year. The organiser's goal is for it to grow to a 10-day event by 2022.[39]

This festival promoted witchcraft and sorcery at the highest of level, all being funded by our government and tax euros, with no shame! It is an abomination taking place at an accelerated pace. And it would not have been able to do so, if we had not let witchcraft into the Church first, with all our different pagan and occultic practices that we, His people do with no shame.

The Holy from the Unholy

1. As His Bride, we need to come low before the Lord, and confess and forsake our sin of welcoming Halloween into our homes, churches, communities and nations.

2. We need to confess and forsake the sin of bringing this filth into the Church, and into our nations through the observance of demons and occultic practices.

3. We need to stand in the gap and confess and ask for forgiveness for the ignorance of those practicing and observing Halloween, in our churches and Christian fellowships, for those Christians who compromise and tolerate such practices. At the same time, asking for the spirit of truth to enlighten the eyes of their hearts' understanding that they would come out of this unholy, pagan worship.

4. We need to humbly pray for God's mercy and deliverance from this filth and abomination that is in our land, starting in our homes and Christian fellowships, while confessing our sin, as His Ekklesia, for allowing it into our government.

5. We need to once and for all close the door of this wicked demon worship in our lives, if we are partaking in it personally.

6. We need to ask the Lord to purify our hearts, minds, souls, homes, churches, ministries, cities and nations through the blood of our Lord Jesus Christ, from every way these occultic powers have polluted, defiled, infected and affected our lives.

7. We need to ask the Lord with a humble spirit, to teach us that we may know the Holy from unholy, the unclean from clean things of God [Ezekiel 44:23].

EZEKIEL 44:23
And they shall teach My people the difference between the holy and the unholy, and cause them to discern between the unclean and the clean.

Other Unholy Alliances

Other unholy alliances that affect our relationship with the Lord, that have found their way into the Church and that we need to abandon: yoga of all kind, and what are known as Flow Yoga classes – for they are rooted in Easter religion. Yoga poses are all offerings to the 330 million Hindu gods. Many Westerners who practice yoga today are unaware that the physical positions assumed in yoga symbolises a spiritual act: worshiping one of the many Hindu gods.[40] Another practice is acupuncture, whose foundation is in Yin and Yang energy that corresponds to 12 meridian points in the human body. Interesting to note, acupuncture was first introduced to Europe about 200 years ago by Jesuit Priests who served as missionaries in the East.[41]

Horoscope readings, fortune telling, Ouija boards and Reiki should not ever be a part of a believer's life. Some of these unholy alliances are more obvious than others, and there are many more. I am only giving a broad stroke overview and not an in-depth review of these practices. There is a lot of information on the internet that you can research that will show you the dark spiritual roots to these practices, that many Christians believe are okay, or have just not ever considered the affect that these unholy alliances are having in their lives.

2 Corinthians 6:17-7:1

Therefore, "Come out from among them and be separate, says the Lord. Do not touch what is unclean, and I will receive you. I will be a Father to you, and you shall be My sons and daughters says the Lord Almighty." Therefore, having these promises, beloved, let us cleanse ourselves from all filthiness of the flesh and spirit, perfecting holiness in the fear of God.

Forgiveness, Deliverance and Freedom

When we come to the feet of Jesus and openly confess and forsake our sins, we will never find shame and condemnation! Instead, we will only find forgiveness, deliverance and freedom with the grace that we need to let go of all books, traditions and false beliefs that want to harm us. AMEN!

CHAPTER 8

BEWARE OF THE FALSE PROPHETS

Then many false prophets will rise up and deceive many. For false christs and false prophets will rise and show great signs and wonders to deceive, if possible, even the elect [Matthew 24:11, 24].

The Apostasy Abounds

We are seeing the darkness increase in the Body of Christ. The apostasy continues to abound all around us, with false anointings operating from false prophets and false teachers, deceiving and seducing many away from truth with false words, signs and miracles – all lying wonders! These false leaders are void of holiness, purity, humility and the fear of the Lord. Apostasy can be defined as falling away from biblical principles.

We are seeing witchcraft increase as never before in our midst – with most unaware of the bewitching and beguiling, that is taking place in many church services and meetings. We are seeing the false unity movement to unite religions gain greater momentum, with the Pope and many charismatic leaders heading this movement, saying that diversity of religions are to unite. There are many false prophets in these last days, saying "Peace, peace" when there is no peace, who are deceiving the masses.

A few years ago, I asked the Lord about this, as many teach and believe that we are to find common ground by putting aside our doctrinal differences, and uniting in His name. But what He told me was, *"Unity in truth,"* meaning that we are to unite in truth. Truth has to be the foundation of everything we do – not walking in compromise just to get along. Truth will always divide light from darkness. We saw this with Martin Luther and the Reformation. He nailed the ninety-five theses to the Roman Catholic Church door, protesting their false teachings, and he broke away from them. Remember, the Lord Himself said, *"Do not think I have come to bring peace, but a sword."*

MATTHEW 10:34
Do not think that I have come to bring peace upon the earth; I have not come to bring peace, but a sword.

Great Division in the Church

This separation was the start of the Reformation. It caused a great division to come into the Church in that day. The protestors – the Protestants, did not allow themselves to be deceived with the false teachings anymore, but stood boldly against the error they represented. And because they did – a split came. That is what the spirit of reformation does. It uproots, plucks up, overthrows and destroys a false foundation, paving the way for a true foundation to be laid. It is fueled by intercessory prayer, and when it comes, it makes correction to that which is in error.

The sword that the Lord spoke about is a sword of truth. It pierces the heart with a call to repentance. At the same time, it circumcises our hearts by cutting away the flesh – that which is impure and unholy in our lives. We must pray fervently for the true Church to arise. For her to come out of compromise – to unite in truth, and for great grace, boldness and courage to confront the doctrines of demons, false prophets and teachings that are rapidly increasing.

The Church is full of wolves in sheep's clothing. If we are not going through the process of purification – pursuing truth, holiness, purity and the fear of the Lord, by denying ourselves and taking up our cross and following the Lamb, we will be deceived in these last dark days that we are living in. The Lord wants no one to be deceived, but He alone is the way, the truth and the life. If we enter through any other door, it will lead us into deception.

JOHN 10:1
Most assuredly, I say to you, he who does not enter the sheepfold by the door, but climbs up some other way, the same is a thief and a robber.

On December 1, 2019, the Church of Sweden, St. Paul's in Malmo, began displaying an 'altarpiece.' A painting titled *'Paradise,'* painted by a lesbian artist. It depicts the Garden of Eden with gay couples covered in fig leaves, with a transgender serpent in between them. This abomination was removed a couple of weeks later. It was not removed because it was an outright blasphemy against a Holy God, but because the church leaders feared it could send an anti-trans message – that transgender people are evil or the devil![42]

As God-fearing Christians, we cannot stand silently on the sidelines looking on as spectators. We must, as believer's in Christ – His true Church, be willing to love not our own life unto death. We must stand up for truth, holiness and purity, while praying for the fear of the Lord to be restored to His Sanctuary. We must stand against the evil that is assaulting our faith, and the Holy One who died for us to be free from all sin and bondage! When we do, we can be assured that division will come – the separating of the wheat from the tares, the sheep from the goats, the clean from the unclean. The dividing lines are now being drawn clearly between those who love truth more than the air they breathe, from those who do not.

Spirit of Brokenness

In early November 2019, during a time of waiting on the Lord, He spoke one sentence to me. *"Man cannot accept a spirit of brokenness until he himself has been broken."* I pondered this for days. Two things that the Lord continues to speak to me about is brokenness – meaning being broken for the Lord, and having the hunger of the Lord. They are intimately connected. Until the Lord had spoken this, though, I had always thought that a spirit of brokenness is what would cause His people to want to be broken for what His heart is breaking for – the sin in our lives, in the Church, in our nations, and to want to pray like our lives depend upon it, because they do!

But what the Holy Spirit revealed was that it is the spirit of brokenness that will enable someone to carry the burdens of the Lord in the fullest measure – in vessels who are fully surrendered. When we intercede, to some degree we have a burden to do so. But the more we surrender our will for His, our prayers will increase, our intimacy with Him will increase, and the hunger of the Lord will increase, causing those burdens to increase in fullness. We will find ourselves consumed with His hunger, wanting only what He wants for our lives.

So, if we are not first broken before the Lord, meaning we have crucified our flesh, we cannot accept that spirit of brokenness, for our flesh will not want it and will reject it. When the Lord spoke this to me, He did not use the word 'receive' but 'accept.' To 'receive' and to 'accept' are two different things. To illustrate the difference, we can hand someone a Bible. When they take it, they have now received it from us. But now it is up to them as to whether they will 'accept' what it contains, and make it a part of their life.

Brokenness Marks a True Prophet

Brokenness will mark a true prophet of the Lord. Not only are they broken for what the Lord's heart breaks for, but they have accepted the spirit of brokenness, enabling them to carry His burden for a nation. Why does God send prophets into nations?

1. As a type of savior [Exodus 13:10, Hosea 12:13].

2. To be a counselor [2 Chronicles 20:3-20].

3. To warn of judgments [Jonah 3:4].

4. To be a protector of God's people [2 Kings 6:8-12].

5. To be a restorer. To restore things that a nation and the Church has lost; righteousness, holiness, the fear of the Lord [1 Kings 18].

6. To be a builder. To help build the house of God [Ezra 5:1-6:22, Hebrews 8:5].

7. To prepare the way of the Lord – prepare for revival [Mark 1:3-8].

Accepting the spirit of brokenness is vital, not only for the true prophets, but for all who belong to the Lord, so that revival can come. If we want revival, we must come to that place of wanting to be broken before Him. Where our hearts break for what is destroying us and our relationship with Him, causing us to come to that place of brokenness with fasting and weeping over our sin, until every hindrance is removed between us and the Lord, and the broken fellowship has been restored.

JOEL 2:12 AMP.
Therefore also now, says the Lord, turn and keep on coming to Me with all your heart, with fasting, with weeping, and with mourning [until every hindrance is removed and the broken fellowship is restored].

This brokenness comes at a high price in our lives, and most in the Church have not been willing to pay that price. Why? It is painful. It requires great grace to want to be broken before the Lord. It is why man cannot *accept* the spirit of brokenness until he himself has been broken. But once broken, we will joyfully *accept* the spirit of brokenness that will enable us to be used mightily in these last days, to bring in the final, great harvest!

Bar Jesus the False Prophet

In Acts 13 we see Bar Jesus, the false prophet who was also called Elymas. He operated under a false anointing that was fueled by witchcraft. Elymas was close with the proconsul – the ruling governor, Sergius Paulus. When the governor wanted to hear the Word of God from Paul and Barnabas, this false prophet opposed them, not wanting the Word of God to come forth. Paul, filled with the Holy Spirit, rebuked him fearlessly and confronted his evil ways, prophesying about an imminent blindness that would come upon him, because of his wickedness. Because of Paul's bold stand for truth – standing against that false prophet face to face, the proconsul became a believer [Acts 13:6-12]. Truth prevailed over the witchcraft that wanted to manipulate, dominate and try to suffocate and silence the true voice of the Lord from coming forth. And because of it, there was a change on a governmental level.

ACTS 13:6-12
Now when they had gone through the island to Paphos, they found a certain sorcerer, a false prophet, a Jew whose name was Bar-Jesus, who was with the proconsul, Sergius Paulus, an intelligent man. This man called for Barnabas and Saul and sought to hear the word of God. But Elymas the sorcerer (for so his name is translated) withstood them, seeking to turn the proconsul away from the faith. Then Saul, who also is called Paul, filled with the Holy Spirit, looked intently at him and said, "O full of all deceit and all fraud, you son of the devil, you enemy of all righteousness, will you not cease perverting the straight ways of the Lord? And now, indeed, the hand of the Lord is upon you, and you shall be blind, not seeing the sun for a time." And immediately a dark mist fell on him, and he went around seeking someone to lead him by the hand. Then the proconsul believed, when he saw what had been done, being astonished at the teaching of the Lord.

Simon the Wizard

In Acts chapter 18, we see Simon the wizard, who was another false prophet, who operated under a false anointing. He was known to have practiced sorcery, boasting that he was great. The people heeded him, and believed that he was exhibiting the power of God. They were dazzled by him for a long time, because he was able to bewitch and beguile them with his skill in magic [Acts 8:9-11]. Sounds like the Church today, that has been bewitched by magic for far too long!

> **ACTS 18:9-11**
> *But there was a certain man called Simon, who previously practiced sorcery in the city and astonished the people of Samaria, claiming that he was someone great, to whom they all gave heed, from the least to the greatest, saying,* ***"This man is the great power of God."*** *And* ***they heeded him because he had astonished them with his sorceries for a long time.***

What once was, is still the same today. The prophetic stream today is grossly polluted and defiled with such men and women, who claim to be moving in the true power of God. They boast of their churches, their ministries, of their gifts and anointings. They offer prophetic 'services' that are geared to seduce the vulnerable, ignorant or erring. One such advertisement came forth from a ministry that is based in Europe. It encouraged people to join their 'Prophetic Encounter Service' that was to include prophetic call-outs and words of healing. People were told to include their name in the comments section when they registered, so that if the Holy Spirit highlights their name, they will receive an 'encounter' from God. Then came the call for money – to sow into this ministry.

Many Merchandise the Gifts

Many today merchandise the gifts and the anointing for personal gain. We saw that with Simon the wizard – the false prophet. After he believed, was baptized, and followed the teachings of Jesus, he then saw the true power of God flow. When the Apostles' laid their hands on others, he thought he could buy the anointing. Why? So that he could lay his hands on others with that same power and receive personal gain, and to exalt his reputation.

Acts 18:18-19

And when Simon saw that through the laying on of the apostles' hands the Holy Spirit was given, he offered them money, saying, "Give me this power also, that anyone on whom I lay hands may receive the Holy Spirit."

And because of it, Peter severely rebuked him, telling him to repent, for he discerned that Simon's heart was impure, regarding why he wanted the anointing:

Acts 18:20-23

But Peter said to him, "Your money perish with you, because you thought that the gift of God could be purchased with money! You have neither part nor portion in this matter, for your heart is not right in the sight of God. Repent therefore of this your wickedness, and pray God if perhaps the thought of your heart may be forgiven you. For I see that you are poisoned by bitterness and bound by iniquity."

When we chase after an encounter and not a relationship with Jesus, we open our spirit to the realm of the occult. We open ourselves up to be deceived by a false anointing. The root of this will be witchcraft operating, known or unknown in a person's life. That false anointing is prideful, seductive and manipulating, with its goal to deceive and destroy God's plans in our lives.

Many Will Come in My Name

The Lord Jesus spoke about this false anointing when He said many will come in My name, saying, "I am the Christ," and will deceive many. For false christs and false prophets will rise and show great signs and wonders to deceive, if possible, even the elect [Matthew 24:5, 24].

For many years I pondered these verses. In particular, how could someone believe another person who says they are 'Christ'? I would often think, that to do so, that deception would have to be so great in order to deceive the elect. Daniel forewarns in these last days that there will be those who are wise and understanding, but will fall and join themselves with those who have deceived them. When I read these verses, they always put the fear of the Lord into my heart – not wanting to be deceived, yet, knowing we are warned that the very elect can fall!

DANIEL 11:33-35 AMP.

And they who are wise and understanding among the people shall instruct many and make them understand, though some [of them and their followers] shall fall by the sword and flame, by captivity and plunder, for many days. Now when they fall, they shall receive a little help. Many shall join themselves to them with flatteries and hypocrisies. And some of those who are wise, prudent, and understanding shall be weakened and fall, [thus, then, the insincere among the people will lose courage and become deserters.

Then a few years ago, I heard someone teach on this very subject, helping me to understand how it would be possible to be deceived in this way. Christ in the Greek, means 'anointed one.' If we substitute 'anointed one' in place of 'Christ' or 'christs' in the above scriptures, it gives us a better understanding.

*'I am the **anointed one**,' and will deceive many. For false **anointed ones** and false prophets will rise and show great signs and wonders to deceive, if possible, even the elect* [AP].

False Anointings

The Lord was not saying that many will come claiming to literally be Him, although some have tried over time. But what He is saying is that there will be many prophets and teachers who *operate in a false anointing* in these last days. We have seen this rapidly increase, especially in the last five years. As the Lord's return gets nearer, we will continue to see the rise of the false prophets and teachers. One reason being that there are many men and women of God, who were true prophets and teachers, but at some point in their walk, they opened the door of their heart to compromise and mixture. This caused them to embrace false teachings that they once opposed.

Some of these men and women of God, who are in the Church today, are more obvious than others in the error they now teach. But most of it is a subtle twisting and distorting of sound doctrine. And, because these once true prophets and teachers have built up large followings over the years, most who continue to follow them will be deceived. Their followers will be deceived because they will have known these prophets and teachers to be ones who were walking upright before the Lord, and will assume they still are doing so. They will not pay heed to the subtle twists of the Word that have become a part of their current teachings.

But most will be deceived, more so, because they do not know the Word of God. They do not make it a point to spend quality time in the Word, in prayer and in the presence of God, waiting on Him knowing His voice, every day. For when we do, we are able to notice the ever so subtle twists in the teachings coming from these once true prophets and teachers, who have now become false prophets cnd teachers. We will see clearly where their teachings do not align with the Word of God, and will not be deceived. Knowing and obeying the Word of God, and being in an intimate, love relationship with the Lord Jesus is vital, if we are not be deceived.

Whom Will We Serve?

False prophets and teachers cause others to follow their dreams and visions. The Lord allows them into our midst to test and to prove our hearts – whom will we serve? Will we serve a voice that tickles our itching ears and makes our flesh feel good? Or, will we serve the voice of the Lord that calls for our flesh to die – for the repentance of our souls, until every spot and blemish has been removed, until Christ has been conformed completely within our soul?

> **DEUTERONOMY 13:1-4**
> *If there arises among you a prophet or a dreamer of dreams, and he gives you a sign or a wonder, and the sign or the wonder comes to pass, of which he spoke to you, saying, 'Let us go after other gods' — which you have not known — 'and let us serve them,' you shall not listen to the words of that prophet or that dreamer of dreams, for the Lord your God is testing you to know whether you love the Lord your God with all your heart and with all your soul. You shall walk after the Lord your God and fear Him, and keep His commandments and obey His voice; you shall serve Him and hold fast to Him.*

During the 2019 Lancaster Prophetic Conference, Brother Sadhu Sundar Selvaraj, founder of Jesus Ministries and Angel TV, shared an excellent message where he talked about a 'new evil order' that will rise up in these last days. It would be similar to the new world order. But it will be a false prophetic order – a system, not just false prophets. It will be an order that consists of: false prophets, false prophetic churches, false prophetic intercessors, false prophetic pastors, false prophetic psalmists – those who are professional singers that are not anointed, but rely on their abilities.[43] Are we prepared for the depth of deception that is coming? Can we discern clearly His voice from all others? If we cannot, we will end up following another voice.

Bethel's World-Wide Influence

Many today are familiar with Bethel Church, in Redding, California. It is almost impossible not to have heard of them, for they have globally influenced the Body of Christ, with their world-wide movement to bring revival. I want to say first and foremost, I believe that most of their followers truly want to know and follow the Lord Jesus with all their heart, soul, mind and strength! What I share is not targeting them or their character. But is a revealing of some of the unsound biblical teachings and practices that are coming forth from the leadership of Bethel.

For those not familiar with Bethel, in 1996 Bill Johnson moved to Bethel to pastor the church that his father had previously pastored. Prior to this move, Bill was a pastor in Weaverville, California. Under Bill Johnson's leadership the culture of the church shifted in how they think about revival. How they think about prophecy and healing. And about being open to different spiritual experiences. With his leadership and this shift, the church had a new 'revival culture.' They not only wanted revival for themselves, but for everyone world-wide. This passion motivates Bill Johnson's heart.

We see this world-wide movement gaining momentum in their different spheres of influence that include: Bethel Church, Bethel Leaders Network, Jesus Culture and Bethel School of Supernatural Ministry. Their Bethel Leaders Network is a group of churches and leaders globally, who are a part of their network. Many promote Bethel's Sozo Healing, that presents itself as an inner healing and deliverance ministry. Jesus Culture, that was birthed in 1999, promotes not only music, but promotes a 'revival theology and practices' for the Church at large. The Bethel School of Supernatural Ministry draws students from around the world, where they are trained to change the culture of the churches that they belong to or are sent to teach in.

So, it is not just about Bethel – one church, but about a world-wide movement that is being inspired by them. There is nothing wrong with wanting revival. We should all be contending for it to come, but contending for it based on sound biblical teachings and practices. For those who follow Bethel, I encourage you to keep your hearts open to these words that are being shared, by seeking the Lord with fasting and prayer that your spirit may bear witness. This is not a tearing down, or a demonising of Bill Johnson and Kris Vallotton, but a revealing of some of their teachings and practices that are not biblically sound, and leading many into error, and especially our youth.

A Balanced Analysis

An excellent video to watch that was done by a pastor who lives in Southern California, is *Bill Johnson's Theology and Movement Examined Biblically*.[44] He presents a balanced analysis of their teachings and practices. Pastor Mike Winger is the featured teacher of *BibleThinker*, an online ministry. He is strongly committed to a careful and thoughtful study of the Bible with a view toward answering skeptics challenges with reason and scripture. What he shares is based on extensive review of actual video clips and quotes from Bethel's leadership. He does not take what they say out of context, but lets the listener hear for themselves. He in no way demonises Bethel or the leadership. He does not tear down their character. In fact, the opposite, he speaks graciously of them.

Yet, at the same time, he brings out their doctrinal errors that are influencing many. His sole focus is to bring forth understanding on what they teach and what they practice, that has inspired this worldwide movement. His purpose is not to attack or defend them, but to find clarity in what they are doing based on the entire Word of God. He shares how this movement got started, how it was engineered to create a 'signs and wonders' momentum, their theology, how they interpret the Bible, and how they perform prophecy and what they believe about healing.

> 2 CORINTHIANS 11:3-4
> *But I fear, lest somehow, as the serpent deceived Eve by his craftiness, so your minds may be corrupted from the simplicity that is in Christ. For if he who comes preaches*

another Jesus whom we have not preached, or if you receive a different spirit which you have not received, or a different gospel which you have not accepted — you may well put up with it!

Bethel's central theological pillar is to filter everything through Jesus. That might sound like good theology, but if we pay closer attention to their teachings, their teaching allows us to ignore all the other clear teachings that are throughout the Bible. Their theology focuses solely on Jesus and His earthly ministry, and ignores everything else. They cite Jesus as the 'standard.' But their standard is too narrow and limited, and not what the Bible teaches. In one of Bill Johnson's teachings he said:

"Jesus Christ is the perfect theology. It is theological immoral to allow anything, any revelation about God that contradicts what you see in the Person of Jesus, to trump your concept of what God is like. How did Jesus handle sin? How did He handle sinners? How did He handle disease? How many storms did He bless? How many times were there life-threatening storms that He would face in the middle of the sea, and He would say go over to that city and destroy them and it will teach them to pray, and they will become more like Me?"[45]

Unbalanced Image of Jesus

The implication being, that if a person thinks God might cause a storm – like a tsunami or hurricane, that is wrong thinking because Jesus did not cause any storm in the physical pages that describes His earthly ministry. This is an example where their teachings bypass the biblical truth that God brings judgments upon mankind. This creates a distorted, unbalanced image of Who Jesus is. Jesus is the same yesterday, today and forever. This false teaching tells us to ignore Jesus' warnings in Revelation 2:22-23, where He says those who follow the teachings of Jezebel He will throw onto a bed of anguish and strike her children dead. Psalm 119:90 says that the entire Word of God is truth – not just a few chapters that depict the Lord's earthly ministry.

PSALM 119:160

The entirety of Your word is truth, And every one of Your righteous judgments endures forever.

Bethel teaches there are *"superior truths but then there are things that are more true."*[46] It is dangerous to think that there are superior truths and less superior truths. It is insincere to take a certain passage of scriptures, exaggerate it, and then use it to discredit all other scriptures that contradict their false teachings. When we pick and choose scriptures to fit our theology, we tread on dangerous ground. We will open ourselves up to a different spirit and preach another Jesus [2 Corinthians 11:4].

Bethel's Prophetic Ministry

Bill Johnson shared how the prophetic started in Weaverville, California. He describes how he was with a group of men sitting around a table. He asked them all to share what they think Jesus would say, if He were to walk in the room at that moment. They all shared what they thought He would say, and when finished, he says, *"Do you all realise you just prophesied?"*[47] He encouraged them all to say what they imagined in their minds, and he then called it prophecy! That is how his prophetic ministry started. Is that prophecy? No. Is it necessarily wrong? No. But it is wrong to call it prophecy. Prophecy comes either from God, Satan or our soul. Jeremiah spoke about this in chapter 23:

JEREMIAH 23:16

Thus says the Lord of hosts: "Do not listen to the words of the prophets who prophesy to you. They make you worthless; They speak a vision of their own heart, not from the mouth of the Lord.

Bethel creates an atmosphere to prophesy whether it is right or wrong. They encourage people to speak falsely and say it is from God. Is some of it right? Yes. But most of what is coming forth is from the throne of man's impure soul, and not from the Throne of God. They allow only prophesies that are encouraging, so even if you get it wrong, at least it was encouraging. This is the mindset behind their teachings on prophecy that encourages error. When we tolerate too much error in our lives, and do not love truth more than our own life, there are consequences, some more serious than others. It is one reason why it is so important that we pray for those in leadership not to be deceived, and for those that are to come out of that deception.

2 Thessalonians 2:3, 9-11

Let no one deceive you by any means; for that Day will not come unless the falling away comes first, and the man of sin is revealed, the son of perdition. The coming of the lawless one is according to the working of Satan, with all power, signs, and lying wonders, and with all unrighteous deception among those who perish, because they did not receive the love of the truth, that they might be saved. And for this reason God will send them strong delusion, that they should believe the lie.

Bethel's Strange Offerings

Other strange offerings that are a part of Bethel's church culture, with some having been introduced by Bill Johnson's wife:

1. Destiny Card Readings: 'Christalignment' is a part of Bethel's community and are the ones who provide these cards.[48] Bethel, through members of their community, use these cards to 'prophesy' and to draw unsaved people to the Lord. They are popular amongst the youth, and are used at new age festivals. There are seven cards to choose from. A quote from their website, *christalignment.org,* states that their cards lead the way: *"Card readings with Christalignment are always followed by the reader taking the client into a deep encounter using a much higher realm. This is the main part of any reading. Often colour is seen and it is in this realm that answers come for poignant life questions that clients have and lives are changed."*[49] Destiny Reading Cards are nothing less than a 'Christianised' version of Tarot Card readings.

2. Grave Soaking or Grave Sucking: This is where someone lays on the grave of a deceased Christian, people like Charles Finney, John G. Lake, in order to absorb their anointing. According to Bill Johnson's wife Beni Johnson, grave-sucking is *'what I do'* in a photo that she posted to her Instagram account in October 2013.[50] Many Bethel students have followed her lead, lying on the graves of great men and women of faith who have gone onto glory, believing they can receive their anointing this way.

Mantles Versus Anointings

Bill Johnson has gone on the record to say that Bethel does not teach grave soaking or grave sucking, despite his wife's open display of such things. But he does say that God told him to honor those that he considers great men of the faith, and that if we honor them, then God can release the same anointing again. It is the reason why he is building a library museum with artifacts from past revivals, that will house items that belong to Kathryn Kuhlman and other past revivalists. God told him that he would then receive their anointing.[51]

I want to say, there is nothing wrong with a museum that will give honor to past great saints. I believe that is noble and pleasing to the Lord. But the motive for why he wants to build the museum is troubling – so that he can receive the anointing of men and women of God who have gone onto glory. In the book, *The Physics of Heaven*, Bill Johnson states:

"There are anointings, mantles, revelations and mysteries that have lain unclaimed, literally where they were left, because the generations that walked in them never passed them on. I believe it is possible for us to recover realms of anointing, realms of insight, realms of God that have been untended for decades simply by choosing to reclaim them and perpetuate them for future generations."[52]

Beloved, you cannot receive someone else's anointing, as Bethel teaches and practices. There is a difference between mantles and anointing – they are not the same thing. A mantle can be defined as: a role, position, function, duty, or responsibility. So, we can receive another person's mantle – have the same call on our lives, so to speak. We see that with the prophet Elijah where his mantle was taken up by Elisha, after Elijah was caught up to heaven [2 Kings 2:13].

But the anointing on a person's life comes from God alone. It is unique for each person. It is what enables them to walk out that call on their life. Many can have the same calling, but how we function in that call will be unique – no two anointings are the same, for only the Lord knows how and who we are to influence. God anoints us according to our call and how we are to function in that call. It takes years for the anointing to mature in a believer's life. It does not happen overnight, and it comes at a high price. If we are not willing to pay the price, we will not walk in that anointing as it was intended. It is not so man can be glorified, but is rather for His Kingdom to come and His will to be done in and through that person's life, all to His glory.

During one of Bethel's services, I watched a well-known woman of God minister, primarily to the youth. She told them that they were to turn to the person next to them, lay their hands on them, and give them their anointing, so they would in effect, have a 'greater anointing.' I was very troubled by what I heard and saw take place. I asked the Lord, *"Is it possible Lord to give someone else our anointing?"* He told me, *"No, the anointing belongs to Me. You cannot give away that which does not belong to you."*

Therefore, what this woman of God was doing, was nothing less than witchcraft. Manipulating her will upon those she was ministering to in that meeting. And those who laid their hands on others and 'transferred their anointing' to them, were doing the same! I believe at some point in her walk, this woman of God opened the door to the spirit of witchcraft, unknowingly, and now was practicing things that are nothing less than of the occult and teaching others to do the same, all the while taking place under Bethel's leadership.

We Trusted You!

Beloved, I have seen first-hand and have heard with my own ears, youth coming against a false leader - one who says he is a prophet. He was their pastor and one who violated their boundaries greatly. I sat in a meeting with them as their advocate, to be a support to them, as they confronted their abuser with truth, all the while walking in great love and humility towards him. They said to that man, *"We trusted you, you are the pastor. We trusted what you told us. We did not question what you did - you say that you see the Lord all the time. But what you did was wrong. You knew it was wrong. You were our pastor – we trusted you."* It was a very difficult situation that I was to be a part of, with my role to bring correction to this so-called prophet and pastor who took advantage of some precious lambs.

We should be grieved by what is happening in many Christian meetings, that are saturated with unholy and profane practices and teachings, all the while polluting and defiling the masses, and especially our youth who are innocent, vulnerable and trusting those in leadership to guide them into all truth. As His Body, we must come together and humble ourselves, seek His face and repent for any unclean and unholy practices that we have allowed into the Sanctuary.

LEVITICUS 10:1-2
Then Nadab and Abihu, the sons of Aaron, each took his censer and put fire in it, put incense on it, and offered profane fire before the Lord, which He had not

commanded them. So fire went out from the Lord and devoured them, and they died before the Lord.

You Will Know Them by Their Fruit

Jezebel was a false prophet and teacher. She was a fornicator who brought fornication into the Church, spiritually and physically. Today, we see it not only with practices that are occultic in nature, but with the all-inclusive false grace teachings. These teachings say that all sin is forgiven at our new birth. That we have no need to repent of sin anymore, and that God does not send anyone to hell. Or, some even go so far as to say that if they do believe in hell, then we can pray people out of hell!

And while Jezebel's false prophetic voice is deceiving many, she tries to silence and discredit the true prophetic voice. The Lord said that we will know the false prophets by their fruit. As false prophets and teachers increase, so too will the apostasy [Revelation 2:20, Matthew 7:15-16, 24:11].

> **REVELATION 2:20**
> *Nevertheless I have a few things against you, because you allow that woman Jezebel, who calls herself a prophetess, to teach and seduce My servants to commit sexual immorality and eat things sacrificed to idols.*

> **MATTHEW 7:15-16**
> *Beware of false prophets, who come to you in sheep's clothing, but inwardly they are ravenous wolves. You will know them by their fruits. Do men gather grapes from thornbushes or figs from thistles?*

Remember that Macaiah in 1 Kings 22, was one true voice against 400 false voices. Elijah was one against 850 false voices. That true prophetic voice is the same, yesterday, today and forever, and it changes not. It will always call individuals and nations back to repentance, truth, holiness, purity, and to the fear of the Lord. While doing so, it will not announce itself, but let others do the announcing. We see this with Macaiah. After Ahab calls forth the 400 false prophets with their false word, Jehoshaphat asks Ahab, *"Is there not another prophet of the Lord whom we may call"* [1Kings 22:6-7]?

We should be careful of those in our midst that like to announce themselves as prophets. A true prophet is clothed and robed in a garment of humility and meekness and will let others announce them. They have accepted the spirit of brokenness and carry the Lord's burdens, with their hearts breaking for what breaks His. Their ministries will speak for themselves. They will be preparing those who are in their sphere of influence for the Lord's soon Second Coming and return. That is the fruit that will come forth from the true prophetic voice.

I AM that I AM Yom Kippur Word

While waiting on the Lord, on Yom Kippur October 4, 2014, I received the following word:

"I AM that I AM and I will be all that I AM to a people who have made themselves ready, to those who have considered Me worthy. To those My former rains and latter rains will be poured upon them – together. What I AM about to do to those shining ones, those burning ones is unprecedented. It is Joel 2:28. It is time for the Morning Star to arise within My people who are not ashamed to take My Name, to be carriers of My Name to the nations.

Yes, gross darkness increases. My decrees have been spoken and judgments are going forth, but I will make a way even in the wilderness, and rivers in the desert to those who are Mine. Beware the false prophets are increasing, but those who are Mine know the Good Shepherd's Voice and will arise against these false ones and put their counsel to shame all for My glory, all for My Kingdom's sake, to save and snatch as many from the fire as possible.

It is a time to be vigilant, sober and ever so watchful in word, thought, deed and prayer like never before. The thief is coming, and to those not ready, not watching, he will plunder them. All that they have will be lost. It is the darkest of times for some and it is the greatest of times for those who have been filling their lamps with oil. I AM coming! To some I will be a terror and dread, to those who are Mine I will be Christ within them, the hope of glory, and will far exceed their hopes, prayers and expectation of what I AM going to do through them in these last days.

Be ever so watchful, be expecting Me. As 'suddenly' as My judgments will manifest on the earth, just as 'suddenly' I AM coming for My Bride and will manifest My glory within her to fight this battle with Me from heavenly ground. Every good gift comes down from My Father above, and I intend to bestow upon My Bride every good gift she needs to labor with one hand and carry her sword in the other, not missing a step, not faltering – but walking with Me, side-by-side. What joy My Bride is to Me. How I long for our Wedding Day where her joy is made complete for all of eternity. I AM that I AM!"

The Lord is looking to His Church – His Ekklesia to govern the affairs on earth as in heaven. He expects us to do so! He never promised it would be easy, but promised to provide everything we need to do it His way, if we are willing. AMEN!

CHAPTER 9

OUR SANCTIFICATION AND CONSECRATION

But we are bound to give thanks to God always for you, brethren beloved by the Lord, because God from the beginning chose you for salvation through sanctification by the Spirit and belief in the truth, to which He called you by our gospel, for the obtaining of the glory of our Lord Jesus Christ [2 Thessalonians 2:13-14].

Earlier, we looked at how king Ahab of Israel was more evil than any king prior. And it was because he married Jezebel a Phoenician – a Canaanite, who caused him to follow Baal and Ashtoreth, by building altars of worship to them. This caused the Israelites to follow these false gods. This mixed marriage to Jezebel was not good. It was lethal to Ahab and to God's people! It caused a lot of sorcery, sexual sin, compromise and unholy alliances to take place within the temple of God. This is why God said he was more evil than any other king.

Elijah confronted Ahab and the Israelites, asking how long they would waver between two opinions. He slew the 450 false prophets of Baal, a great victory, but he failed to slay the 400 false prophets of Ashtoreth. Because of it, Elijah ran for his life in fear of Jezebel! Elijah quickly descended from Mount Carmel – a place of great victory, to find himself in the wilderness wanting to give up and die [1 Kings 19:4].

But then an Angel of the Lord came to him, telling him to arise and eat, for the journey was great. The food that Elijah ate carried him on a 40-day's journey to Mount Horeb. To a place of desolation. To a place of brokenness before the Lord. In Hebrew Horeb means desert. The root of Horeb is *'charab'* and it means: be desolate – to be in ruins.[53]

Desolate and Utterly Broken

It was in the wilderness, in a place of feeling desolate and utterly broken where Elijah could hear the voice of the Lord again, after Jezebel tried to destroy him with fear. And what he first heard was that he was not where he was supposed to be – hiding in a cave, in fear wanting to die. And secondly, that he was not alone. For the Lord had 7,000 others who would not bow to Jezebel and her false prophets [1 Kings 19:13, 19]!

Despite Elijah's moments of weakness, he confronted sin boldly. He would not have been able to do so, if he did not live a lifestyle of sanctification and consecration unto the Lord. I used to think the two – sanctification and consecration were interchangeable, until the Lord gave me greater understanding about them several years ago. They are intimately connected to working out our salvation with fear and trembling [1 Philippians 2:12].

If we do not want to be bewitched and beguiled by these workers of darkness that are in our midst, and if we want to be prepared to be the Bride of Christ – one who will be dressed in our wedding garments, then we must live a life of sanctification and 100% consecration. That will only come about if we deny ourselves, take up our cross and follow the Lamb wherever He may lead. For the only way to the glory is through the Cross.

The End Result of Faith

Before I share about sanctification and consecration and why they differ, we need to understand that our salvation is not complete at our new birth. When most in the Church hear salvation, they think it means a person is saved, and that is all that it means. But being saved is just the first step of a Christian's journey – without it we could go no further in His plans. It would be more helpful and accurate to say our salvation has stages that we walk through. With the goal being that we would receive the end result our faith, the salvation of our soul [1 Peter 1:9].

1 Peter 1:9

Receiving the end of your faith — the salvation of your souls.

1 Peter 1:9 AMP.

[At the same time] you receive the result (outcome, consummation) of your faith, the salvation of your souls.

By this verse we can see there is a beginning and an end to our faith. Therefore, there is a beginning and an end to our salvation. That end is the salvation of our soul – or for our soul to be completely purified. That is the main reason why God gave us faith to begin with – so that we would come into the fullness of our salvation, causing our souls – our minds to be renewed – transformed, until Christ has been completely formed within us.

At our new birth we have the Seed of Christ inside of us, and we are a new creation with His DNA, but that Seed is in its infantile stage. It has to grow and mature. And that Seed grows and matures, when we allow our soul to be 'saved' meaning to be purified from our sin nature. For at our new birth, our souls were not saved [James 1:21].

James 1:21

Therefore lay aside all filthiness and overflow of wickedness, and receive with meekness the implanted word, which is able to save your souls.

James is talking to believers in this verse, not the unsaved. So, it is vital that we understand our salvation was not complete once we got saved. It is complete in the sense that it is a finished work on the Cross, and every provision that we need to come into the fullness of that finished work has been given to us. But it is not complete in that we do not tangibly have the full stature of Christ developed into our souls at our new birth. We are not yet manifesting that fruit in our lives. A portion of it, yes. But not the fullness of it.

It has always been the Father's plan that we would grow and mature in Him, until we have the full stature of Christ within us. Until we become mature Sons of God, for He desires for us to rule and reign with Him – but it is not automatic. Just like a good father would not give his child a car and let them drive it without first taking lessons to know how; nor would he without them passing their test that provides the license that is needed, and qualifies them to drive it [Job 1:6, Ephesians 4:13, 1:5, Revelation 21:7].

So like a good earthly father, our Father in heaven is not going to let us rule and reign with Him, in the fullness of our rightful inheritance that can only be found in Him, until we have learned to become like Him, in our words, thoughts and deeds.

REVELATION 21:7
He who overcomes shall inherit all things, and I will be his God and he shall be My son.

Three Main Stages to Salvation

This earth is our training ground to learn to reign with Him, by overcoming the obstacles He has left in our path, His way. For it is those who overcome and become mature sons of God, who will receive the full inheritance from the Father. So getting saved is the first step to becoming a mature Son of God. That first step, when we receive Jesus into our heart, gets us out of hell, if we do not fall from grace later on our walk. It is a free gift – there is nothing that we can do to earn it! We can see in 2 Thessalonians 2:13-14 there are three main stages to our full salvation:

2 THESSALONIANS 2:13-14
*But we are bound to give thanks to God always for you, brethren beloved by the Lord, because God from the beginning **chose you for salvation** through **sanctification** by the Spirit and belief in the truth, to*

*which He called you by our gospel, for the **obtaining of the glory** of our Lord Jesus Christ.*

First Stage: Justification

The first stage is justification. We are justified by faith and the redemptive work of the Cross – His blood atones for our sin. We are saved by believing in our hearts that God raised Jesus from the dead and confess with our mouth that He is Christ and that His blood atones for our sin. This is the first stage of our salvation, which all new believers in Christ comes to.

> ### ROMANS 3:24, 28, 10:9-10
> *Being justified freely by His grace through the redemption that is in Christ Jesus, therefore we conclude that a man is justified by faith apart from the deeds of the law. That if you confess with your mouth the Lord Jesus and believe in your heart that God has raised Him from the dead, you will be saved. For with the heart one believes unto righteousness, and with the mouth confession is made unto salvation.*

Second Stage: Sanctification – Our Purification

The second stage is sanctification. It is the purification stage. It is the process where our soul gets saved by the renewal of our mind. Primarily, by how we respond or react to the trials, afflictions and suffering that we all go through in life. Every believer should be walking through this process. Our trials were not meant to destroy us, but to be redemptive and transform us, if we respond according to the spirit and not react according to our flesh. Remember, this earth is our training ground, so we do not want to waste our tears!

This is the bigger part of a believer's journey. It becomes a lifestyle of choices we make every day, whether or not to surrender our will for His will, according to the Word – according to His ways, and not man's. Mind and soul, for the most part, can be interchangeable in scripture. And our mind or soul, could be likened to a computer hard drive. It is what stores our personal data. Our wounds, offenses with others. It is where we store unhealed trauma from horrible things that have happened to us as children, that have caused us to see God and others through a distorted lens.

Or, could be things that happened while in our mother's womb before we were born – like addictions, bitterness, or being involved in the occult. For those things can affect the choices we make, which cause hurt to us and others. Our soul is where our impure motives – jealousy, greed, bitterness, and pride are stored and kept hidden in darkness.

It is why Paul tells us to be renewed in the spirit of the mind, and to present our bodies as a living, holy sacrifice – the call to live the crucified life. We are not to be conformed to this world, but to be transformed by the renewal of our mind, so that we will know the perfect will of God in our lives.

EPHESIANS 4:23, ROMANS 12:1-2
And be renewed in the spirit of your mind. I beseech you therefore, brethren, by the mercies of God, that you present your bodies a living sacrifice, holy, acceptable to God, which is your reasonable service. And do not be conformed to this world, but be transformed by the renewing of your mind, that you may prove what is that good and acceptable and perfect will of God.

Without Transformation We Stagnate

Renewal of our mind is vital for transformation to take place in our lives. The Lord wants transformation to take place in our lives daily. Without it, we will stagnate. We will not grow and mature into the fullness of His stature. Transformation is vital if we are to know the perfect will of God. If we are not going through stage two, this purification process, we will make decisions based on the unhealed wounds and deceptions of our soul. We will walk after our flesh and not after the spirit. We will miss the high call that is on our lives to know Christ – to share in the fellowship of His sufferings, so that we would be transformed to His death. Why? So that we can know the power of His resurrection!

PHILIPPIANS 3:10
That I may know Him and the power of His resurrection,
and the fellowship of His sufferings, being conformed to
His death,

A resurrection can only take place after a death. If we are not willing to die to our needs, wants and desires – our will, we will not be filled with His glory, which is what transforms us by one degree to the next [2 Corinthians 3:18]. The Lord longs to pour His glory into us. But it is not automatic. To the degree that we are willing to be empty of ourselves, is the degree to which He can fill us with His glory. If He filled us with His glory in our unrefined and impure heart condition, it would kill us. He cannot mix His holiness with our filth.

My Awakening

In 2007, in the early morning hours, I experienced my first interactive vision, where I was allowed to live and see some events of these last days that we are living in. It shook me to the core, causing such fear to come upon me, that I could not leave my house. Not because I was afraid of immediate danger, but because I knew that what I had just been allowed to experience was reality, and that when I looked around my bedroom and surroundings, I knew it was not reality – it represented a false sense of security. I did not want to lose the 'reality' of what I had been allowed to experience, or to step outside into the world that says all is okay, when the reality is that everything is not okay, and most are not prepared for what is coming.

I was so shaken by what I saw that I kept asking the Lord, *"Lord, how do I prepare for what is coming? How would I ever survive something like that? And to be honest, who would want to survive something like that?"* At that time, I was not seeking the Lord about the last days. I was a very ordinary Christian, and just praying for the needs around me. Over time, the Lord gave me other visions about the last days, and the tribulation that is coming on this earth. Again, I was not seeking such encounters. At that time, this was all new to me. I did not know what to do with them, nor to whom should I even share them, fearing that others would think that I was crazy. I did not even know how to pray about them but hid them in my heart and never forgot them.

High and Holy Standards

Then in August 2009, the Lord came and awakened me in a different way. It was not a pleasant awakening either, as the Lord was revealing His high and holy standards of what it means to be pure in His eyes, and just how pure one's heart has to be if they are to see His face. After having that encounter with Truth, I was shaken to the very core of my being again and devastated. I felt like my relationship with the Lord was in the gutter, even though at that time, I thought I was a 'good' Christian. I would have never considered myself backslidden. I was pursuing Truth to the best of my ability and was obeying the Word of God. But then Truth came that one night, and the reality was this: if the Lord had come for me in that moment of reckoning, He would not have taken me as His Bride, and I would not have seen His face. It was a very painful, troubling time that followed, as I felt I was starting my relationship with the Lord all over again.

For about a year following this experience, the Lord in His loving mercies, kept revealing how He saw my heart – my thoughts, my motives, the words I spoke, my actions in detail, the way He did. It was ugly, it was black and it was painful. And remember, this is one who was not backslidden, who was not in some hidden secret sin, but was thinking all was okay in my relationship with the Lord. When in reality, according to Him, it was not okay.

To add to my pain, others in the Church, my family and most friends could not understand what was happening in my life, and to them, what seemed liked 'radical changes' were taking place. And because they did not understand, they would say things like, *"God would never expect anyone to go through, or ask you to do what you are doing."* It was a lonely, misunderstood time, where I was often judged harshly by those who were not willing to heed the Bridegroom's Voice to become His Bride.

The Narrow Road

But how wrong they were: not only would He do so, but He also expects us all to want to be purified to His standards. His Word calls it: 'living the crucified life.' I have been crucified in Christ, it is no longer I that lives, but Christ lives in me [Galatians 2:20, 1 Corinthians 15:31, Philippians 1:21]. This means to deny yourself, take up your cross and follow the Lamb wherever He may lead, which involves a total surrendering of our will for His. We are all called to live this life – it is the narrow road that leads to life. It is the only path that will lead to the glory – to be His Bride, one who will rule and reign with Him for all of eternity. But it comes at a high price, and most in the Church are not willing to pay that price.

This only all caused me to pursue the One I love more fervently than ever before. During this time, the Lord brought me through an intense accelerated period of purification. It was an Isaiah 6 *"Woe is me, for I am a man of unclean lips!"* time for me, where I fell on my face in tears, often broken to pieces. But I was determined to allow the Lord to do all that He desired to do in me, as I could not bear to be anything less than all that He wanted me to be – His Bride. Nor was I willing to have anything less than all that He had planned for me – both the suffering that He had called me to endure, as well as the glory that He wanted for me, which was to live in Him and with Him, on this earth and forever. When I share this with others, it is what I describe as my awakening. It was the call and the beginning of my journey to become His Bride.

He Will Tolerate No Mixture

Almost exactly a year later, in August 2010, one day during my time of prayer, the Lord came. He spoke to me about His Church, letting me feel His displeasure while He spoke, *"How filthy she was. How so few will be His Bride as His Bride will be without spot or wrinkle. They think they can mingle the Holy with their filth. I AM the Holy One Who sits in the highest heavens and I can only mingle with the pure."*

I was stunned! The fear of the Lord fell upon me. After a time of silence, not knowing if the Lord was done speaking or not, I was about to get up off the floor, but fell back just as quickly and cried out, *"Lord, I am so sorry, I do not need to be anywhere today, if you have anything else you wish to speak to me, I am here."* He then gave me the call upon my life and said, *"I want you to teach My people what it means to be pure."*

When the Lord spoke that, I cried and cried and cried. Saying, *"Me, little miss black heart – the one that You have been showing how black my heart has been. How could I ever teach Your people what it means to be pure?"* I did not know at that time, but it was the very reason why He chose me for such a call. Because I was willing to sit in His Refiner's fire no matter how ugly, hot, or uncomfortable it felt. I did not look for a way out but let Him do what He wanted to accomplish in my soul, no matter how painful, or how much it cost: with my reputation, time, finances and relationships.

No Price Too High to Pay

There were times where I thought I would die from the embarrassment of my sin that nobody could see but Him! And then He would ask me to confess my sin to those I had wronged: to confess my actions or thoughts that were impure and unjust before Him and ask for their forgiveness. So as He showed me, I would humble myself before Him and others, confessing my sin. I would make amends wherever and whenever He showed me. I learned to be quick to repent and quick to obey. For I only wanted to know Him and please

Him. I just had to be His Bride, even if it meant that I might die in the process of trying – everything else paled in comparison. There was no price too high to pay, He is worthy of it all!

It is why often others hear me say that it will cost you everything, if you are to become the Bride of Christ. There is much misunderstanding about what God requires, and what costing us everything really means. Luke chapter 14 versus 26-27 and 33 will help guide our steps in what it means to be a true disciple of Christ.

Make no mistake that our Great King's standards are high and holy. Not everyone will qualify to be His Bride. He is not going to share His Throne with a harlot – with those who have other lovers. If we are not willing to sit in the Refiner's fire until all the impurities and dross of our soul has been removed, we will disqualify ourselves. He is not looking to disqualify anyone, but instead, He has given us all the grace that we need to allow this process to take place in our lives. But most will disqualify themselves by the choices they make. For most want to hold onto their own life, and are not willing to lose it, that they may find it [Matthew 16:25].

If we are to be His Bride, we need to be making ourselves ready. The Marriage Supper of the Lamb is for a Bride who has made herself ready on this earth, today. It is not something that happens once we leave this earth – that once we get to heaven, we will all then become the Bride. We have a very active role to play, every day, every choice we make [Revelation 19:7-8].

Overcoming through Relationship

Thank God for Jesus – for His grace and long suffering towards us that none should perish. Thank God for the grace He provides that enables us to overcome all He has left in our paths to overcome, so He can qualify us to become the Overcomers, the Bride of Christ, the Sons of God. For it is only the Overcomers who will sit next to Him on His Throne [Revelation 3:21]. Our overcoming comes about through relationship – an intimate relationship with the Lover of our soul. For ultimately, He longs to restore us back to that same place of intimate fellowship that He shared with Adam and Eve in the Garden, in the cool of the day before the fall of man. But He cannot have that same intimate fellowship that He had with Adam and Eve, with vessels who are unclean, and who are full of the world's ways of doing things.

So we get to decide if we will walk through this stage of purification or not. It is often painful, lonely, at times confusing, with many humblings along the way to extract out of our soul those things that harm our relationship with the Lord, and with others. A key to walking out this stage in our walk, is that we are obedient to truth. When we do, it causes the Holy Spirit, the Sanctifier to purify our soul causing us to become more like Jesus – to be perfected in His love.

> **1 PETER 1:22 AMP. | AP**
> *Since by your **obedience to the Truth through the [Holy] Spirit you have purified your soul** for the sincere affection of the brethren, [see that you] love one another fervently from a pure heart.*

We see also that the Holy Spirit is given to those who obey truth – that it is not automatic to receive the Holy Spirit just because we say we are a Christian:

> **ACTS 5:32**
> *And we are His witnesses to these things, and so also is the Holy Spirit whom God has given to those who obey Him.*

Third Stage: Glorification

The third stage is glorification. As we walk through stage two, our soul gets purified. We become more like Jesus in word, thought and deed. As we behold Jesus, meditating on the Word, and living a lifestyle of prayer, our mind will be renewed. Our soul will be transformed by one degree of glory after another being filled with His Light. We become more compatible with His divine nature.

2 Corinthians 3:18
But we all, with unveiled face, beholding as in a mirror the glory of the Lord, are being transformed into the same image from glory to glory, just as by the Spirit of the Lord.

We move further away from the lust of the eyes, the lust of the flesh, the pride of life – from the spirit of the world, and move more towards truth, purity, holiness and into a deeper, more intimate walk with the Lord. It does not mean we are there yet, because we are not. But we are now walking on the narrow road that leads to life. The things of this world no longer attract us. For we have fallen into His transcendent love trap that has captivated our souls. Where turning back to our former habits, or lifestyle is no longer desirable to us, no matter how hard the narrow road can be to walk upon at times.

Matthew 7:13-14
Enter by the narrow gate; for wide is the gate and broad is the way that leads to destruction, and there are many who go in by it. Because narrow is the gate and difficult is the way which leads to life, and there are few who find it.

These are the three main stages of salvation that He desires every Christian to go through. That we would behold Him, so that we will become like Him, until we are completely transformed into His image and likeness and that we could come into union with Him. Sadly, most Christians today do not get past stage one. It is why we have seen so little transformation in believers' lives. They have either no desire to know Him and to go onto glory, or, they have been wrongly taught that it is automatic. It is impossible, though, to go onto stage three – glorification – to be the Bride of Christ, if we are not willing to go through stage two, the sanctification and purification process. Remember that Esther was only allowed to enter into the king's house after twelve months of purification [Esther 2:12, 17].

Salvation is a Process

So, salvation is a process – a journey. At our new birth, the Lord could have saved our soul when we became a new creation. In our finite reasoning, we could say that would have made it so much easier for Him and for us! But in His infinite wisdom, He saw our end from the beginning and He said it was very good. He wants all to be the Bride of Christ, but that positioning in Him will only come to those whom He has qualified as an Overcomer. It will come to those who overcome life's adversities by letting their afflictions mold and shape them into His likeness.

So He alone knows what we need to reach that end. In the journey of transformation, He left our soul in the unsaved – impure state to draw us out of darkness and into His Light. He did this to draw us into a deeper, more intimate, love relationship with Him. Another reason is that He will not go against our free will. We get to decide how much we will know Him to become like Him.

While on this journey of transformation, He will ask many times, *"Will you forgive those who have betrayed you? Will you let Me comfort your broken heart, when the losses are so great and more than your heart can bear? Or will you run to man and this world to find comfort?"*

Will you keep crying out, *"Search my heart, O'God, and keep showing me every wicked thing that is within me – everything that hinders me from going forward in Your plans?"* Will you trust Him to take care of you, when all you have ever known in your life are people who have abandoned you? Maybe from birth, you were given up for adoption. Maybe a marriage, where your spouse left you for another. Will you still believe He is good all the time, and that He has your best interest at heart, despite your oceans of tears and mountains of heartache? Will you believe that He is able to take that which was meant to destroy you and turn it and work it for your good?

Will you stay in the wilderness, that dry barren and lonely place as long as He requires, that you may find the Lover of your soul? Or, will you run and try to find and an escape route because the pain feels like more than you can bear – or the losses are just too great to face?

Or, because your pride exalts itself over His humility and plans for your life? Will you try to rescue, defend and preserve your own life, when unjustly accused? Or will you let your Redeemer rescue, recover and restore all that has been lost, stolen and destroyed in your life His way, and in His timing? He desires that we would come to that place where we no longer rely on self, or man to meet our needs anymore, instead that we would rely solely on Him to direct our steps. Despite our weakness' and failings, we must trust that He is able to prevent us from stumbling and to present us blameless before the presence of His glory, in triumphant joy.

Exposing the Tares

When we go through sufferings, it exposes the tares of our hearts – sin, wrong thoughts, hurts, that all need to be uprooted. But He will not do this uprooting against our will. That is why they have been left intact, so to speak, at our new birth – not because He is cruel, unkind, or forgetful – the opposite is true. He created us to co-partner with Him, and He longs to work out those things that are destroying our soul together. Not to shame and condemn us – but to set us free from them!

For nobody cares more about our soul being saved and our destiny being fulfilled than He does! He is fighting for us, and not against us. Yet, He wants our will to come into alignment with His in every area of our lives. That takes time. It means developing and maintaining an intimate, mature relationship with Him. It is a wonderful journey – it is worth any price we may have to pay. When we go through this purification process His way, I promise you, you will not have one regret! And along the way, He will become your constant companion Who you cannot bear to be apart from, but instead, you passionately desire for Him to live through you!

But it does not happen overnight – just like an earthly relationship, it takes time to grow and mature. Nor is it automatic to be the Bride of Christ, such that all Christians will reside in the Holy of Holies sitting next to Him on His Throne, to rule with Him in the Millennium Reign. Sadly, most Christians will end up in the outer courts of heaven, furthest away from His Throne. This is because they were not willing to follow the Lamb wherever He may have led. They were not willing to pay the price – to die to their selfish ambitions, needs or desires. Most will have wasted their trials and the one life they have been given to become perfected in love. That is not His desire for anyone. Instead, He has called us all to go onto perfection – to spiritual maturity, which Paul spoke of in Hebrews.

HEBREWS 6:1 AMP.
Therefore let us go on and get past the elementary stage in the teachings and doctrine of Christ, advancing steadily toward the completeness and perfection that belong to spiritual maturity...

Sanctification and Consecration Work Together

As we walk out the three stages of full salvation: justification, sanctification and glorification. We can see that stage two – our sanctification and purification, is where we will spend a lot of time working out our salvation with the Lover of our soul. While doing so, sanctification and consecration will work together to bring about His eternal plans, purposes and desires in and through us. So, how does sanctification and consecration differ?

Sanctification is: a work that only the Holy Spirit can do within us. When we repent of sin, the Sanctifier of truth comes and cleanses us from that sin. We cannot do that work, only He can. It positions us to keep making choices of consecration, moving us more and more towards truth, holiness and purity.

Consecration is: the lifestyle choices that we make to follow and obey truth, to be pure and holy. In its simplest form, it means to be set apart to something. That can be either good or bad. In a believer's life, it is the everyday choices that we make to be set apart for God's purposes to manifest in our lives.

Many people have consecrated themselves – set themselves apart, to be like this world. Therefore, it is a choice that we make to be separated to something that is either good or evil, and used for those purposes in our lives.

1 PETER 1:15-16
*He who called you is holy, **you also be holy in all your conduct**, because it is written, "Be holy, for I am holy."*

Both have the meaning to be separated, and the two work together. You cannot have one without the other. Consecration comes when we make a choice to be separated, holy unto the Lord in an area of our lives. It is not always sin that we need to turn from. Often, it is simply are we willing to let go of this world's ways of doing things?

Are we willing to let go of distractions, no matter how well meaning they can appear, but are stopping us from fulfilling His eternal purposes for our lives? To the degree we are willing to consecrate our lives, will be to the degree we can be filled with the glory – we will decide by our lifestyle choices, for He will not go against our free will.

How We Spend Our Time

One example could be how we choose to spend our time. We may decide to no longer watch a certain TV show. Or, you may choose to get rid of your TV and choose instead to spend that time in worship or prayer. When we make such choices, we are consecrating ourselves. We are setting ourselves apart to be holy unto the Lord in that area of our lives.

About ten years ago, after my husband had died, I was on a 40-day fast. During that time, I had purposed not to watch a 30-minute TV show that I used to enjoy watching with my husband, and instead to spend that time in worship. The TV show was not evil in content. It was about real people buying houses. So I spent that time in worship. And when I ended the fast, I could hardly wait to eat my favorite foods, while watching this TV show. After about 10 minutes, I was not enjoying this time at all, and told the Lord, *"I need You more than I need to watch this show."* That was the last time I watched that show, and soon after quit watching TV altogether. I would then spend my evenings in worship and prayer.

During those 40-days, though, I noticed His presence had increased tangibly, but I did not feel that different outwardly. I had no idea how much He had purified my soul during this time of consecration, until I sat down to watch that TV show 40-days later. So, while I had made the choice to give up that TV show, He had done a work in that area of my soul that I had yielded, and it caused my spirit to grow. And when I came back into contact with the things of the world – that TV show, I no longer had a desire for it. Instead, I had a holy dissatisfaction for it! I could have kept watching that TV show, as it was not sin to do so. But it was stopping me from changing from one degree of glory to the next. I had a taste of just how good His ways were, and it caused me to have no desire to go back to my old ways. That is His goal for all of us – for the world that has stained our souls to be removed, so that Christ can be completely formed within us.

The Sanctifier is at Work

Initially, we may not feel any different when we make choices to live a more consecrated life unto Him. But I can assure you that the Sanctifier is at work – cleansing that area of our soul that was polluted by the things of this world and filling it with His Light. It is His Light within our soul that causes it – our mind, to be renewed and transformed into His image and likeness, by one degree of glory to the next. For every time we surrender an area of our lives – by choices we make, an impartation of the Living God – Who is Light, enters that area of our soul, sanctifying and purifying it. It causes that part of our soul to be transformed, so we become more like Him.

That is how sanctification and consecration work together. It begins with a choice we make. And behind every righteous choice is the power of God to perform it. For He gives us the desire to do what is right – to want to be pure and holy, and then He works that into our soul.

PHILIPPIANS 2:12-13

Therefore, my beloved, as you have always obeyed, not as in my presence only, but now much more in my absence, work out your own salvation with fear and trembling; for it is God who works in you both to will and to do for His good pleasure.

Both sanctification and consecration should be happening in a believer's life every day. In our walk, we should be constantly moving more towards holiness, and further away from sin, wrong thoughts and impure motives. We should be moving further away from the lusts and pleasures of this world. If we keep moving towards holiness, we will reach the end result of our faith – the salvation of our soul.

In every decision we make, we decide whom we will serve this day – our flesh with its finite reasoning, or the Lamb of God's infinite wisdom, Whose ways are not our ways. Every day, we get to decide if we want to embrace compromise in our homes, churches and ministries – or whatever our sphere of influence may be, at the cost of our souls being saved.

A Call to be Pure

2 TIMOTHY 2:20-21 AMP.

But in a great house there are not only vessels of gold and silver, but also [utensils] of wood and earthenware, and some for honorable and noble [use] and some for menial and ignoble [use]. **So whoever cleanses himself** *[from what is ignoble and unclean,* **who separates himself from contact with contaminating and corrupting influences] will be a vessel set apart** *and useful for honorable and noble purposes,* **consecrated and profitable to the Master,** *fit and ready for any good work.*

So we have a call to action on our part. It is a call to come out of the unclean things and those things in our lives that are not profitable to our soul and to His Kingdom. So, we have our role to make those choices to do so. And then there is His role, to sanctify and purify our soul, when we make those choices that align with His will for our lives.

> **2 Corinthians 6:16-7:1**
> *And what agreement has the temple of God with idols? For you are the temple of the living God. As God has said: "I will dwell in them and walk among them. I will be their God, and they shall be My people." Therefore, "Come out from among them and be separate, says the Lord. Do not touch what is unclean, and I will receive you. I will be a Father to you, and you shall be My sons and daughters says the Lord Almighty." Therefore, having these promises, beloved, let us cleanse ourselves from all filthiness of the flesh and spirit, perfecting holiness in the fear of God.*

We see Paul give that call to action on our part – to remove the idols of our hearts and to separate ourselves from that which is unclean, so that holiness can be perfected in our lives. For the Lord wants to dwell within our soul and walk amongst us, by filling us with His glory. But He cannot do so, if we are not willing to come out of those unclean things that are contaminating our soul and crowding Him out. He can only increase when we decrease.

Do We Love Truth?

In these last days, it is vital that we come to that place where we love truth more than the air we breathe and pursue it as if our lives depend upon it. For if we do not, we will easily be bewitched and beguiled, and especially by those who are wolves in sheep's clothing. How much we love and pursue truth is intrinsic to our sanctification and consecration.

John 14:6 says, He is the way, the truth and the life. Every time there is a reference to Jesus in the Bible, we could exchange His name for truth, for He is truth. He is not a truth, but Truth itself! John 14:15 says, "If you love Me, keep [obey] My commandments." Or, we could say, "If you love **Truth** [Jesus], then obey **Truth** [Jesus]."

JOHN 17:16-17 AMP.

*They are not of the world (worldly, belonging to the world), [just] as I am not of the world. **Sanctify** them **[purify, consecrate, separate them for Yourself, make them holy] by** the **Truth; Your Word is Truth.***

So how do we learn to love truth? By the washing of the water of the Word. The Word sanctifies – purifies us. When we read and meditate on it, it becomes a part of our soul. It will convict us of sin, teach us righteousness and forewarn of judgments. Every time we read our Bible, we are making a choice to consecrate ourselves unto Him, and the Sanctifier is at work within our soul, whether we feel it or not. So, if we love Him [truth], we will obey Him [truth]. Obedience to truth is vital to being sanctified, and to be able to receive and understand revelation.

1 PETER 1:22 AMP. | AP

*Since by your **obedience to the Truth through the [Holy] Spirit you have purified your soul** for the sincere affection of the brethren, [see that you] love one another fervently from a pure heart.*

It is our obedience to truth that causes the Sanctifier, through the working of the Holy Spirit, to purify our soul. 1 Peter 1:22 reveals how our consecration – separating ourselves unto Him by obeying truth, brings sanctification to our souls. It is a solid, foundation and roadmap for us to follow that will bring us to the end result of our faith – the salvation of our soul.

So, in our journey to full salvation, we see that the Lord has His role to Sanctify us. That He is the Sanctifier, Who sanctifies our soul through the Holy Spirit, when we make choices that align with truth. At the same time, we see that we have our role. And our role is to surrender our will in all situations and count it all joy, by giving thanks while doing so! That we are to love and obey truth as if our lives depend upon it, because they do. And to meditate and behold the Word of God, with a lifestyle of prayer. With the goal that we would receive the end result of our faith, the salvation of our soul, until our soul has been completely conformed to the image of Christ.

Our Soul Needs Renewed

So it is not automatic for every believer to attend the Wedding Supper of the Lamb – to be the Bride of Christ. Getting out of hell is free, but to be the Bride will cost us everything. The Lord is looking to qualify us to be the Bride, not disqualify us. We decide how holy and pure – set apart we become by whether we live a consecrated life unto the Lord, or unto this world.

The traps and enticements of this world can easily cause us to lose our way. Ungodly movies and computer games, gambling, smoking, foul language, anger, unforgiveness, romance novels and other books that are full of the world, pornography and all other sexual sin, lying, gossiping, grumbling and complaining are just a few of the things that trap and ensnare our souls. Every Christian will have to pass through Galatians 5:19-21, with the goal to not have any of the works of the flesh manifesting in our lives.

GALATIANS 5:19-21 AMP.
Now the doings (practices) of the flesh are clear (obvious): they are immorality, impurity, indecency, Idolatry, sorcery, enmity, strife, jealousy, anger (ill temper), selfishness, divisions (dissensions), party spirit (factions, sects with peculiar opinions, heresies), Envy, drunkenness, carousing, and the like. I warn you

beforehand, just as I did previously, that those who do such things shall not inherit the kingdom of God.

As we come out of those unclean places, we should see an increase of Galatians 5:22-23. We will be able to see the Lord is taking what was meant for our harm and working it for our good! But it requires our response every day. It has to be intentional, if we want to possess our full inheritance and to be an Overcomer [Philippians 3:14-16, Revelation 3:21].

GALATIANS 5:22-23 AMP.
But the fruit of the [Holy] Spirit [the work which His presence within accomplishes] is love, joy (gladness), peace, patience (an even temper, forbearance), kindness, goodness (benevolence), faithfulness, Gentleness (meekness, humility), self-control (self-restraint, continence). Against such things there is no law [that can bring a charge].

Suffering = Transformation

When we go through tests and sufferings by denying ourselves, our soul – or mind gets renewed. It is one of the main reasons why God allows suffering in our lives. For it exposes sin, with our character flaws and weaknesses that need to be perfected and strengthened. So the Sanctifier can come and purify those areas with truth, causing us to be more like Him in word, thought and deed.

We see so few, though, who teach and preach the true Gospel that Jesus, Paul and the Apostles preached – the crucified life. And for those who are teaching it, their church or ministry numbers are not large, because those who hear it are not willing to die to self. They love their flesh and this world more than truth and are satisfied with their carnal Christian life. It is why we see so little transformation taking place in the Body of Christ, meaning our character becoming Christlike in our words, thoughts and deeds.

Not helping us to die daily, are the false grace messages that say we do not have to die! That Jesus wants us happy and prosperous all the time. That He suffered, so we do not have to! These teachings are shallow, selfish and void of truth. They cater to man's flesh and not to the saving of man's soul. Messages like these deceive, weaken and stop His Church from engaging in the battle. They do not help prepare the lambs and sheep for these last days we are living in. For they believe and teach "Today we eat, drink and marry, for tomorrow we die and we will all go to be with Jesus."

If we are not willing to crucify our flesh, we will not only be deceived and unprepared for what is coming, but we will stay stuck in our misery with very little transformation in our lives. So many believers are stuck in a lifestyle of addiction, anger, jealousy or sexual sin. Things we hate and are ashamed of, but have not been able to overcome them, to the point we believe the lie that it must be normal to be like this.

If that is you, be encouraged today and allow the sanctification process to work in your life. You do this by repenting of whatever your issue is, and then make the choice to resist it – deny yourself, as often as needed. Ask the Lord to strengthen you – to give you the grace to overcome. Do not let Satan hold your mind captive, saying what a failure you are when you slip. Or, you will never change, so why bother? Our soul does not get renewed overnight, but by one righteous choice at a time. Every time we make a righteous choice, the power of God is working to set us free!

To be Sanctified Wholly

1 THESSALONIANS 5:23
Now may the God of peace Himself sanctify you completely; and may your whole spirit, soul, and body be preserved blameless at the coming of our Lord Jesus Christ.

When we do our part, the Holy Spirit and the God of peace will sanctify us wholly. He starts bringing oneness to our spirit, mind and body. There is a 'rest' that we come into, when we understand and yield to this process. It can be painful, humiliating, lonely and confusing. To those around us, our lives may look like a mess, or they think we are crazy because they judge us by this world's standards, and not by what the Word teaches and what God expects of us.

But when we yield, we have a peace that surpasses all understanding because we will know we are in the perfect will of God. Especially, when we walk though very painful situations. We will know He is after something in us – to become like Him in word, thought and deed. We will know that He wants us to overcome the adversity, His way – that we would fulfill the high call that is upon our lives, to be His Bride. All are called, but few are chosen [Matthew 22:14].

Seven Spirits of the Lord

So why is it so vital that we go through the purification process? Because it is His answer for the last days we are living in – to have a Bride on this earth, before the Lord's Second Coming and return, who will have made herself ready. One who is without spot or wrinkle. One who will have no other lovers but Him and will be equally yoked to her Bridegroom King in word, thought and deed. One who has been completely emptied of self, so that vessel can be filled with His glory – the Seven Spirit of the Lord, that Isaiah 11:2 speak about.

ISAIAH 11:2
The Spirit of the Lord shall rest upon Him, the Spirit of wisdom and understanding, the Spirit of counsel and might, the Spirit of knowledge and of the fear of the Lord.

That is His answer for these last days. The Seven Spirits of the Lord operating in pure vessels, who will destroy the lethal combination of the spirits of Jezebel and Ashtoreth. A company of people on the face of this earth that will be filled with the knowledge and the glory of the Lord, as the waters cover the sea, who will finish what Elijah failed to do.

They will destroy all the witchcraft works of Jezebel that are operating in the Church, and will be used mightily to bring in the great harvest.

Beloved, we do not have much time left before the Lord's Second Coming and return, and the Church is not ready. At large, the Church today is no different than when it was in Elijah's time. When he came on the scene there was much darkness in Israel: idol worship, false prophets, false religions, Ashteroth and Baal worship with their wicked temple prostitution.

Love of This World

If we are really truthful, we would have to confess we have lots of idols – a lot of other lovers that we willingly give our love, affection and time to – love of mammon, love of this world. Our homes, services and meetings are full of the world and its ways of doing things. The Lord told us that if we have love for this world and the things that are within it, we cannot love the Father. We cannot have it both ways. The Kingdom of God is black and white, and there is no grey – it is one or the other [1 John 2:15].

1 John 2:15
Do not love the world or the things in the world. If anyone loves the world, the love of the Father is not in him.

The Church, at large, is saturated with temple prostitution. With many bringing their idols – lust of the flesh, lust of the eyes and pride of life, with them every time they go to a church meeting. How can this be? Because we have lost the fear of the Lord, and have embraced the fear of man, wavering between two opinions. Sin is no longer boldly confronted in the pulpit, as it was with Elijah. Instead, it is tolerated and promoted under a spirit of false unity. Very few leaders are calling for repentance and teaching those in their midst to be holy and pure, set apart and consecrated solely unto the Lord and His holy purposes. Very few are teaching His people the difference between the profane and the holy.

King Ahab was very corrupt, and Jezebel was more corrupt. She killed the prophets, replacing them with the false prophets who ate at her table of idolatry. She is a false prophetess who is seducing God's people to go astray with false teachings [Revelation 2:20]. Jezebel rules in most churches and ministries today. She comes to kill the true prophets, or to kill a true prophetic church or ministry. She comes to seduce a prophetic pastor or leader into sexual sin: leaders beware – Jezebel is not always a woman! She has many masks that she can hide behind. False prophets and teachers are on the rise with doctrines of demons infiltrating the Church.

Warrior Bride Arise!

But there is good news for those who are making themselves ready. The Bride of Christ – the Overcomers, the Sons of God, will arise in these last days and destroy Jezebel once and for all. But she will not go without a fight – she loves her power and hates being confronted! But the Bride of Christ will be a Warrior Bride with hands trained for war! She will know how to labor with one hand and how to effectively wield her sword in the other. Remember, Jesus did not come to bring peace on earth, but a sword. That sword is truth and it is being restored. That sword will separate the wheat from the tares, the sheep from the goats. It will be the purification of the Church that Daniel 12:10 speaks of during the great tribulation.

DANIEL 12:10
Many shall be purified, made white, and refined, but the wicked shall do wickedly; and none of the wicked shall understand, but the wise shall understand.

This is the hour we are in. This is a work for the End-times Army of God to complete – to destroy the works of Jezebel. But too many sons and daughters of the Most High God have fallen into the destructive grips of Jezebel. It is time for the Bride to arise, and not only destroy her works, but set the captives free from Jezebel's bondage of sexual immorality and idol worship.

But first, we must get free from those areas in our lives that are holding us captive. It is why this process of sanctification and consecration is vital to our walk. Why it needs to be a part of our daily lives, until every spot and blemish has been removed. Until His love has been perfected into our souls. Until it is no longer about us, but all about Him. Until His holy hunger and desires have been satisfied in and through us, even if it costs us our lives. For the Lamb deserves to receive the reward of His suffering in the fullest measure. It has to start with us – for that is all we can offer Him – ourselves as living sacrifices, to be used for His glory.

In the days to come, the storms are going to be coming fast and furious. What we have walked through in 2020 is just the beginnings of Him shaking everything that can be shaken, so that the only thing that will remain is that which cannot be shaken, starting in His Church. He wants no one to be deceived, but everyone to be prepared.

To Know His Voice

To be prepared, we must abide in the secret place of the Most High. We must abide in His love – for that is the secret place of the Most High. For when we abide in His love, we become like Him in our words, thoughts and deeds, and no evil can touch us! To be prepared, we must know the voice of God in our lives. If we are to know His voice, then we must die daily, so our soul can be purified and our mind renewed. Otherwise, we will not know His Voice. We will end up making decision based on our soul – our flesh, and not our spirit. Our soul will work with our flesh against the will of God for our lives. Instead of our soul and spirit working together to make the will of God known to us. We will not be prepared instead led astray and miss His plans.

We need to remember always, that becoming love is the goal – it is what will bring us to the end result of our faith. For faith works through love [Galatians 5:6]. The two working together is what will cause our soul to reach the fullness of our salvation. It is what will give us the grace, strength and courage to be conformed to the image of Christ. This will come by embracing our trials and afflictions and letting them transform us, and not destroy us, and by learning from our mistakes. We must learn everything that the Master Teacher wants us to learn while we still have time.

Otherwise, we will be like the foolish ones who built their house on sand to their utter destruction. We will be like the five foolish virgins who did not fill their lamps with oil, and when they wanted to enter the Marriage Supper of the Lamb, it was too late. They heard those dreadful words, *"I do not know you"* [Matthew 7:26-27, 25:1-12].

When the hurricanes are blowing, the earthquakes are shaking and fires are breaking out all around, if we have not learned to abide in His love and to hear the voice of the Lord, like Elijah in that place of consecration and brokenness, we will look at the storm clouds around us, and not hear what the Lord is speaking to us. We will not be where we are supposed to be.

Murder in My Heart

A few years ago, I went through a fiery trial of affliction, where a relationship fell apart. It had been made known to me that the source of this affliction was witchcraft that had been put upon the relationship wanting to destroy it. While walking out this trial, I was called to a 40-day fast. During these 40-days, I had a dream where I had known a murder had taken place. And when someone brought it to my attention, I did not think there was anything wrong with it – it did not phase me in the least! When I awoke, that really bothered me. I said, *"Lord, what are You saying? What is that about?"* I was so bothered that I thought it was okay to kill someone!

A few days later, while pondering that dream before the Lord, He showed me that I had murder in my heart towards one of the persons involved in this relationship. That after months of feeling betrayed, the pain of it, and the relationship never getting resolved, and being blamed for it all, I was starting to get bitter. My heart was starting to get hard towards this person. Not on a conscious level, for I truly desired restoration, despite how much I had suffered.

1 JOHN 3:15
Whoever hates his brother is a murderer, and you know
that no murderer has eternal life abiding in him.

But the Lord was showing me that I was now a murderer! I just cried, asking for much forgiveness! I did not want my heart to become hard. The Lord is so jealous over us – so faithful to show us our faults, kindly and not by beating us over the head.

I Would Have Missed Him!

At the end of that fast, the Lord told me that if I had not obeyed Him and set that time apart to fast those 40-days, I would have missed Him! I would not have realised the sin of murder that was in my heart. He did not mean that I would end up in hell, which we can if we do not repent of any unforgiveness, hate or murder in our hearts. But for where He was taking me, that sin, if it had been allowed to continue any longer, it would have blinded me, and would have caused me not to hear His voice correctly.

Even though I made many mistakes during this trial of affliction, I learned a lot through my suffering. And despite the times I thought I was going to die; the Lord was perfecting that which concerns me – the purification of my soul. He was bringing me the correction and humility that I needed. Despite Satan wanting to destroy me, all things were working together for my good, even if I could not see or feel it. I clung even tighter to the only One, Who truly cares about my soul being saved and my destiny being fulfilled.

ROMANS 8:28
And we know that all things work together for good
to those who love God, to those who are the called
according to His purpose.

When relationships fall apart, it is not always what it may seem. There are real forces of evil working against them. And at the same time, if we are going through the purification process, we can be encouraged knowing that the Lord is working all things for our good. That during our sufferings, He is refining those areas of our soul that need to be refined, and would not have if we had not gone through those difficult situations. Equally, when we walk through these hard places in our different relationships, we need to be fighting for each other and not against each other. For we cannot afford to take one single offense with one another. If we do, we not only hurt ourselves, but those whom we are called to work with in these last days. It is possible to miss the plans He has for us.

To Hear His Voice Clearly

So Beloved, without going through the sanctification and consecration process, we will not see our faults that need correcting. We will not be willing to be corrected. We will not be able to hear the Lord's voice clearly. In these last days, we cannot afford not to hear His voice clearly. These workers of darkness are real. They hide behind many different masks and their root is witchcraft. They come to destroy any way they can and not just us, but the eternal relationships that we are to have with each other. One of our greatest weapons of warfare against them, is to sit in the Refiner's fire and go through the purification that will enable us to be armed and prepared. So we can fight against their evil from higher ground, where unoffended love never fails!

ISAIAH 48:10 AMP.
Behold, I have refined you, but not as silver; I have tried and chosen you in the furnace of affliction.

If we are to be ready for our Wedding Day – to be the Bride of Christ, to be the Overcomers, we need to be going through the purification process. We need to stop wavering between two opinions. We need to put away all compromise and mixture by making choices to be holy, separated unto Him, until the God of peace makes us whole. It is vital if we are to be prepared for the dark days ahead. He wants to qualify us to be an Overcomer, but we have to decide whom will we follow. I ask you this day: how long will you waver between two opinions?

The Lord will tolerate zero mixture. He is coming back for a Bride who has made herself ready – one without spot or wrinkle. We get to decide, every day in the choices we make. We saw what happened when Ahab allowed mixture into his life – it opened the door for deception, bringing him to utter ruins.

GALATIANS 5:9
A little leaven leavens the whole lump.

If the Lord is God then follow Him, whole heartedly, but if Baal then follow him [1 Kings 18:21, Jer. 29:13]. AMEN!

CHAPTER 10

YOURS IS THE KINGDOM –
NOTHING CAN STAND AGAINST IT

Yet in all these things we are more than conquerors through Him who loved us. For I am persuaded that neither death nor life, nor angels nor principalities nor powers, nor things present nor things to come, nor height nor depth, nor any other created thing, shall be able to separate us from the love of God which is in Christ Jesus our Lord [Romans 8:37-39].

While writing *The Good Shepherd's Heart: Living Parables*,[54] I had a glorious encounter with the King of Glory while on one of our many prayer walks! I was left in holy awe of our fearsome and fearless great, Conquering King! It forever changed how I see His Kingdom and His Light, and just how true it is that nothing can stand against it – no evil, no darkness, it must flee!

I had returned from several days of travel and ministering. After unpacking and passing physical and mental exhaustion hours prior, I could not sleep. My physical body was done, my mind was done, but my spirit was more alive than ever and won over as I was being pulled into a place of worship around 2 A.M. I stayed in that place until about 4:30 A.M. when I finally went to bed. I remember waking at 7:30 A.M. too tired to get up, and slept until 9:30 A.M.

After brushing my teeth, washing my face and making a cup of tea, I was anxious to be with the Lover of my soul and headed for the prayer room. As I sat before Him, my whole body felt drained, yet I was longing to go for a walk as it had been days since our last walk.

After some time in prayer, I just had to go for a prayer walk and felt the Lord's pleasure in this. He knew I was weak in so many ways and how our walks refresh me, especially when I feel so drained.

I wanted to be with just Him – not even necessarily to pray with Him, but to just be with Him, to be in His company – to have a good family chat, or the long comfortable pauses that come in a relationship that has matured, where you just enjoy each other's company without having to say anything.

With those thoughts, I left the prayer room and got ready to leave. I had many ministry administrative needs pulling at me. I thought that maybe I should review one of the meeting messages that I had just completed while walking, or I should keep praying as we have so much to pray for as a ministry.

As I was contemplating all of this, what quickened my spirit was to abandon both those plans and to just worship Him! To worship Him to the one song, *What a Beautiful Name*,[55] which He had given me several days ago. So, I grabbed my iPhone with my worship music playlists and earbuds, and a little before 11:00 A.M., I headed out the door. I was so looking forward to this time of just being with our Beloved Yeshua in song!

It was a beautiful late morning, the sun was breaking through the clouds, and the wind was refreshing, not too cold. I was marveling at His creation all around me – it is always a beautiful sight to my eyes and spirit. I told the Lord, *"I think we should go on the walk that takes us to the high place."* It's about a two-hour walk that passes the farmlands, up the hills to open land which is surrounded by mountains and hills, with a view of the valley and sea below.

As I was worshipping, my spirit became more and more alive, and I wanted passionately to worship Him and proclaim His greatness, His glory, His Kingdom to anyone around me! Yet at the same time, everything within me wanted to bow before His glory – He was overwhelming my senses, and it only made me want to worship Him more fervently! I soon forgot my fatigue, for every part of my being was awakened to His glorious presence.

Soon into our walk, I became very aware of the Lord's tangible presence, as He was walking alongside me on my right. I only wanted to tell Him how much I loved Him, adored Him – how He is worth everything! He then spoke some words to me that melted my heart and I started to cry. At the same time, I could not stop worshipping Him!

As I did, I could clearly perceive in my spirit that the Lord and I were not alone. His holy angels were on our left and right and slightly behind us. I felt the glory and majesty of the Lord, as I have experienced on one other occasion. How it feels to walk alongside the Lord of lords and King of kings, and at the same time the Lover of our soul; how high and noble His heart is and how His Majesty commands for all of creation to worship Him. It caused me to fervently worship Him even more.

As we continued our walk, and as I worshipped, His presence increased to the point He was now letting me see something I had never seen before. It is hard to describe in human words, but He was increasing His Kingdom all around me and letting me see just how glorious and powerful it is to the measure I was able to behold it in that moment. Even though my natural eyes could see fields, trees, roads to my right and left, my spiritual eyes were opened, and I could see His holy array gathering around us.

2 KINGS 6:16

Do not fear, for those who are with us are more than those who are with them.

At first, what I could see was the increase of His holy array around my immediate surroundings. It was glorious and astounding – I was speechless and in awe! The more I worshipped, especially when I sang the chorus of that song,

You have no rival, You have no equal,
Now and forever God You reign,
Yours is the Kingdom, Yours is the glory,
Yours is the Name above all names,

What a powerful Name it is,
The Name of Jesus Christ my King,
What a powerful Name it is,
Nothing can stand against it,
What a powerful Name it is, the Name of Jesus.

He kept increasing His Kingdom around me, as more and more of His holy array gathered.

Every time I sang, He kept increasing to the point when we reached the high place – the open land before me, behind me, the valley and sea below was completely covered with His holy array – His angels! I was quickly becoming more undone yet unable to stop worshipping Him! As I looked all around me – 360 degrees – as far as my eyes could see it was all His glorious Kingdom, and at the center of it all was the Lord Yeshua!

As we walked, the manifestation of His beautiful, glorious, majestic presence – His Light and glory went before us. As He moved, it not only moved with Him, but His power and Light increased! He was allowing me to stand right next to Him in the center of it all! How can one describe the beauty of His holiness and the awe of His power?

What He wanted me to see was just how powerful His Name and His Kingdom is – how nothing can stand against it! Darkness cannot even get close – His Light literally pushes it back. I could now understand the very words He had put in my heart to sing so many days ago on a Kingdom level – *Yours is the Kingdom, Yours is the glory, what a powerful Name it is – nothing can stand against it!*

This position in Him – this protection, is for all who will follow Him wholeheartedly. For all who will pay any price to be one with Him. For those who will deny themselves, take up their cross and follow the Lamb wherever He may lead, who will not love their own life unto death. For those who will be found without spot or wrinkle. This is the glorious position His Bride will have in Him to accomplish His will in the dark days ahead.

What also came to mind in that moment, was the scripture He had put into my heart a couple of months ago to meditate on daily:

Colossians 1:9-11
I pray that you may be filled with the knowledge of His will, with all wisdom and spiritual understanding, that you may walk worthy of the Lord, fully pleasing Him, being fruitful in every good work, increasing in the knowledge of God. Strengthened with all might, according to His glorious power, for all patience and longsuffering with joy.

He was letting me see and feel how His glorious power strengthens us with all might, and how those who are for us are far greater than those who are against us. We all know the scripture, right? I can assure you that this day it took on a whole new meaning to me, enlarging my spirit! I stood in awe, gazing all around me, undone, and thanking Him for allowing me to have this experience with Him. It will forever change how I see the battles that we as believers are called to not only walk through but are expected to overcome by being love and Light.

I could only shout as loud as I could, for all to hear, just how worthy He is! How He is worth everything – any price one may need to pay to be found to walk worthy of Him – to be able to be positioned in that place of glory in Him where nothing can stand against the eternal kingdom plans He has for us. To be able to crown Him with the honor that belongs to Him alone.

Beloved, we are in a serious spiritual battle against darkness that wants to stop His Light from coming forth in our lives. It wants to stop His Kingdom from being formed within us, in our loved ones, in our families and in our cities and nations. This darkness wants to stop us from fulfilling our high and lofty destiny that each of has in Him.

If you are facing dark times, battles within and without, be encouraged and assured that those who are for us are far greater than those who are against us. Now is the time to surrender all and let His Refiner's fire come and do the purifying work within your soul, so that the darkness within can be replaced with His love and Light.

This encounter not only forever changed how I see His Kingdom and His Light, and just how true it is that nothing can stand against it – it changed how I pray!

Romans 8:31

If God is for us, who can be against us?

I promise you, if you are willing to let go of the things that are hindering the plans your Good Shepherd and the Lover of your soul has for you, you will not regret it! May you hear the Good Shepherd's voice calling you closer to His bosom – calling you to become love and light. He is calling you to push back the darkness that wants to destroy you, your family, and the eternal plans that He has for you!

Be assured though, it will cost you everything, but you will find there is no price too high to pay to be the Bride of Christ – positioned in Him, in His glory to rule and reign with our Great King Jesus for all of eternity! AMEN!

ENDNOTES

1   Merriam-Webster Online, s.v. "complacency" https://www.
merriam-webster.com/dictionary/complacent (accessed
October 16, 2020). Author's paraphrase included.

2   Merriam-Webster Online, s.v. "bewitched" https://www.merriam-
webster.com/dictionary/bewitched (accessed October 16, 2020).

3   Merriam-Webster Online, s.v. "beguile" https://www.merriam-
webster.com/thesaurus/beguile (accessed October 16, 2020).

4   Nita Johnson, *Prepare for the Winds of Change II, The Expanded
Vision,* (Clovis, CA: Eagle's Nest Publishing 1991, 1994, 1997,
1998) 186.

5   Charles Dickens, *Tale of Two Cities*, originally published 1859.

6   January 2017, *European Parliament website*: https://www.
europarl.europa.eu/doceo/document/A-8-2017-0005_EN.html
(accessed May 18, 2020).

7   Dr. Judy Mikovits, PhD and Kent Heckenlively, JD, Plague of
Corruption, (Skyhorse Publishing, Inc. April 14, 20200).

8   May 19, 2020, Steve Barick, *Have Ye Not Read?* Article: *Occult
Ritual Transformation and Coronavirus: How Mask Wearing,
Hand Washing, 'Social Separation' and Lockdowns Are Age-Old
Occult Rituals Being Used to Initiate People Into a New Global
Order, https://haveyenotread.com/occult-ritual-transformation-
and-coronavirus/* (accessed July 21, 2020).

9   February 4, 2019, *Vatican Website*: http://w2.vatican.va/
    content/francesco/en/travels/2019/outside/documents/
    papa-francesco_20190204_documento-fratellanza-umana.html
    (accessed February 9, 2019),
    Prophecy News Watch: https://www.prophecynewswatch.com/
    article.cfm?recent_news_id=2952#WP3qF4ZfVjZqvspb.99
    (accessed February 9, 2019).

10 March 29, 2018, *National Catholic Reporter*:
    https://www.ncronline.org/news/vatican/vatican-claim-pope-
    denied-hells-existence-unreliable (accessed May 18, 2020).

11 November 22, 2019, *Catholic Culture.org*:
    https://www.catholicculture.org/news/headlines/index.
    cfm?storyid=44200 (accessed May 18, 2020).

12 Reported February 12, 2018, *TruNews*: https://www.trunews.
    com/stream/the-dark-side-of-davos-the-witch-and-the-cardinal
    (accessed May 18, 2020).

13 August 2, 2017, *Chicago Tribune*: https://www.chicagotribune.
    com/business/blue-sky/ct-wisconsin-company-microchips-
    workers-20170801-story.html (accessed May 18, 2020).

14 October 22, 2018, *NPR*: https://www.npr.org/2018/10/22/
    658808705/thousands-of-swedes-are-inserting-microchips-
    under-their-skin (accessed May 18, 2020).

15 May 3, 2020, *theJournal.ie*: https://www.thejournal.ie/hse-
    contact-tracing-app-coronavirus-5090759-May2020/ (accessed
    May 3, 2020).

16 *Behind the Name*, https://www.behindthename.com/name/
    jezebel (accessed July 23, 2020).

17 Sadhu Sundar Selvaraj, *Elijah is Coming*, (Singapore: Jesus
    Ministries Pte Ltd. 2018), 220.

18 Sadhu Sundar Selvaraj, *Elijah is Coming*, (Singapore: Jesus Ministries Pte Ltd. 2018), 221.

19 Sadhu Sundar Selvaraj, *2019 Lancaster Prophetic Conference,* August 15, 2019 message.

20 Dr. Katharine Zappone, *The Hope for Wholeness: A Spirituality for Feminists*, (Twenty-third Publications 1991).

21 July 3, 2018, GCN, https://gcn.ie/irish-priest-filmed-gay-sex-church-altar-takes-personal-leave/ (accessed July 26, 2020).

22 Sadhu Sundar Selvaraj, *Elijah is Coming*, (Singapore: Jesus Ministries Pte Ltd. 2018).

23 Mulinde, John Wilfred, *'Opening the Portals of Prayer,' Combat in the Heavenlies* - Book 1, 2005, 2015, World Trumpet Mission, (subheads added and inserted by author).

24 Pat Holiday and Bishop Samuel Vagalas Kanco, *The Witch Doctor and The Man City Under The Sea*, (Agapepublishers, Jacksonville, Florida 2001).

25 Pat Holiday and Bishop Samuel Vagalas Kanco, *The Witch Doctor and The Man City Under The Sea*, (Agapepublishers, Jacksonville, Florida 2001), 47-49.

26 June 4, 2020, *Forbes*, Article: *#28 J.K. Rowling*, https://www.forbes.com/profile/jk-rowling/ (accessed July 30, 2020).

27 March 4, 2012, Mission Evangelism, *The Harry Potter Books are Witchcraft*, Updated March 4, 2012, http://harrypotterpower.com (accessed July 30, 2020).

28 July 1, 2000, Ian Potter and Vikki Potter, quoted in Danielle Demetriou, *Harry Potter and the Source of Inspiration*, Electronic Telegraph, *The Harry Potter Books are Witchcraft*, Updated March 4, 2012, http://harrypotterpower.com (accessed July 30, 2020).

29 October 20, 1999, J.K.R. interview, National Public Radio, *The Harry Potter Books are Witchcraft*, Updated March 4, 2012, http://harrypotterpower.com (accessed July 30, 2020).

30 Richard Abanes, *Harry Potter and the Bible: The Menace Behind the Magick*, (Christians Publications, US, 2001), 24.

31 J.K. Rowling, *Harry Potter and the Sorcerer's Stone*, (Scholastic Press, 1998), 297.

32 August 15, 2004, *J.K. Rowling interview, Edinburgh Book Festival*, January 7, 2019, Laurel Geggel, *LiveScience, Here's Where J.K. Rowling Got Her Magical Ideas, for Harry Potter*, https://www.livescience.com/64427-harry-potter-history-of-magic-photos.html (accessed July 30, 2020).

33 Pastor David J. Meyer, The Last Trumpet Ministries, Article: *The Witchcraft of the Narnia Chronicles*. C.S. Lewis, *The World's Last Night and Other Essays*, (Harcourt, Brace and Company, New York, 1959), 98-99.

34 Pastor David J. Meyer, The Last Trumpet Ministries, Article: *A Former Witch Looks at The Lord of the Rings*.

35 Pastor David J. Meyer, The Last Trumpet Ministries, Article: *A Former Witch Looks at The Lord of the Rings*.

36 *Samhain (Smain) The Celtic Roots of Halloween*, https://www.newgrange.com/samhain.htm (accessed August 3, 2020).

37 Rev. D.A. Waite, Tract: *Halloween, The Devil's Birthday*, (The Bible for Today, Collingswood, New Jersey).

38 Faithful Word Publications, Tract: *What's Wrong with Halloween*, (Arabi, Louisiana).

39 January 12, 2019, thejournal.ie, *An iconic, bucket list experience': Major international Halloween festival set for Meath this year*, https://www.thejournal.ie/halloween-meath-festival-4428496-

Jan2019/, https://www.pucafestival.com (accessed August 3, 2020), https://www.dunboynecastlehotel.com/puca-dunboyne. html (accessed August 3, 2020).

40 Dr. Laurette Willis, *Praisemoves Fitness Ministry*, Article: *Yoga Poses Are Offerings Hindu Gods? Why Yoga and Christianity Don't Mix*, https://praisemoves.com/about-praisemoves/why-a-christian-alternative-to-yoga/yoga-postures-are-offerings-to-hindu-gods/ (accessed July 31, 2020).

41 Let Us Reasons Ministries, Article: *Acupuncture-Acupressure*, http://www.letusreason.org/Nam10.htm (accessed July 31, 2020).

42 December 13, 2019, Serena Sonoma, *Out Magazine, Article: Church Removes LGBTQ+ Artwork Over Fears It May Be Transphobic, https://www.out.com/art/2019/12/02/church-sweden-artwork-replaces-adam-and-eve-gay-couples* (accessed August 4, 2020).

43 Sadhu Sundar Selvaraj, *2019 Lancaster Prophetic Conference*, August 15, 2019 message.

44 February 13, 2018, Pastor Mike Winger, *Bible Thinker Online Ministry*, https://www.youtube.com/watch?v=r3tEv26OMTU (accessed March 24, 2019).

45 February 13, 2018, Pastor Mike Winger, *Bible Thinker Online Ministry*, Bill Johnson quote, https://www.youtube.com/watch?v=r3tEv26OMTU (accessed March 24, 2019).

46 February 13, 2018, Pastor Mike Winger, *Bible Thinker Online Ministry*, Bill Johnson quote, https://www.youtube.com/watch?v=r3tEv26OMTU (accessed March 24, 2019).

47 February 13, 2018, Pastor Mike Winger, *Bible Thinker Online Ministry*, Bill Johnson quote, https://www.youtube.com/watch?v=r3tEv26OMTU (accessed March 24, 2019).

48 January 5, 2018, *Bethel Statement Regarding Christalignment*, https://www.bethel.com/about/christalignment/ (accessed July 31, 2020), June 2, 2019, The Geoffrey Grider, *Clarion Sound*, Article: *Christalignment Chaos At Bethel Church Using 'Destiny Reading Cards' To Deceive Followers With Witchcraft*, https://www.theclarionsound.com/apostasy-the-great-falling-away/christalignment-chaos-at-bethel-church-using-destiny-reading-cards-to-deceive-followers-with-witchcraft/ accessed July 31, 2020).

49 "Our cards lead the way," https://www.christalignment.org/destinyreadingcards (accessed August 9, 2020).

50 Beni Johnson, https://dynamitepublishing.com/2014/08/02/beni-johnson-posts-another-photo-of-herself-on-instagram-in-cemetery/ (accessed August 7, 2020), https://churchwatchcentral.com/2019/04/10/bethel-and-their-apostolic-grave-sucking-culture-still-continues/ (accessed August 7, 2020).

51 Bill Johnson, https://bewatchful.org/2016/10/26/bill-johnson-addresses-some-of-the-controversies-concerning-bethel-church/ (accessed August 7, 2020).

52 Judy Franklin & Ellyn Davis, *The Physics of Heaven*, (Destiny Image Publishers, Shippensburg, PA, 2012).

53 *Strong's Concordance*, H2717.

54 Tracy Hogan, *The Good Shepherd's Heart: Living Parables*, (Manifest International, LLC, 2019), 15-19.

55 Lyrics from song, *"What a Beautiful Name,"* by Hillsong Worship, version author listened to is from *One Event Worship Team One Event 2017*.

ABOUT THE AUTHOR

Ever since the return to the love of her life, the Lord Yeshua, in 1999, Tracy Hogan has walked closely and intimately with the One whom her soul loveth and adores. In 2007 she had a life-changing experience where the Lord allowed her to witness some end-times events. In 2009 the Lord came and awakened her in a different way, by revealing His high and holy standards of what it means to be pure in His eyes and just how pure one's heart has to be if they are to see His Face. It jolted her to the core. It was the beginning of her journey to become His Bride.

Tracy's call is to the nations. She prophetically teaches the Word of God to help prepare the Bride of Messiah for the Lord Yeshua's soon coming return. For her to know how to dress herself in her wedding garments – to be a Bride who has made herself ready – one who will be without spot or wrinkle, and one who will be ready for her wedding day. This bridal preparation comes by teaching her truth, purity, holiness, and in helping nurture in her an intimate love relationship with our Bridegroom King through worship, intercession and warfare.

Tracy resides in Ireland, where she founded *The Voice of My Beloved – A Call to the Nations Ministry*.

OTHER BOOKS BY TRACY HOGAN

The Good Shepherd's Heart: Living Parables

The Voice of My Beloved

A Call to the Nations Ministry

www.thevoiceofmybeloved.com

www.ingramcontent.com/pod-product-compliance
Lightning Source LLC
Chambersburg PA
CBHW051510030726
47592CB00006B/2201